Around Newcastle and Tyneside
in the 1970s

David Morton

iNostalgia

For my parents who provided me with a wonderful childhood during the 1970s

Time is a gypsy caravan
Steals away in the night
To leave you stranded in dreamland
Distance is a long-range filter
Memory a flickering light
Left behind in the heartland
NEIL PEART

Dave Morton has worked in North East journalism since 1989.

Today, he writes on all things retro for ncjMedia which incorporates the Newcastle Chronicle, Sunday Sun and Journal newspapers, and the ChronicleLive website.

A history graduate with a lifelong passion for the subject, he is also a drummer, music fan, and long-suffering Newcastle United supporter. In no particular order, he likes beer, curry and cycling. He is also a dad.

His first book, Newcastle In The Headlines, was published in 2015.

Thanks to my many contributors and all those who have helped me in my 'day job', especially Trevor Ermel, Paul Perry, Norman Dunn, Steve Ellwood, David Dunn and Ray Marshall. Thanks also to the staff of Newcastle Chronicle and Journal past and present. And, most importantly, eternal thanks and love to the people I go home to at the end of every working day, Maria and David.

ISBN 978-1-84547-249-8

©2018Photographs ncjMedia and Trinity Mirror ©2018 Text David Morton

Published by iNostalgia Ltd, Progress Centre, Charlton Place, Ardwick, Manchester M12 6HS, UK

Introduction

Likely Lad Rodney Bewes, left, with writer Ian Le Frenais at St James' Park, checking out a range of outside locations for the upcoming new series, July 1972

At 8.30pm on Tuesday, January 9, 1973, sandwiched between the film Doctor At Large and the Nine O'Clock News, BBC1 unveiled its new comedy series - Whatever Happened To The Likely Lads?

The first episode was titled Strangers On A Train, with the Radio Times informing us: "Bob hasn't spoken to Terry for five years. Then one evening..."

The pair in question were old pals Bob Ferris, as played by Bradford-born actor Rodney Bewes, and Terry Collier portrayed by James Bolam who hailed from Sunderland.

The series was the sequel to an original 1960s black and white offering.

The new 1970s all-colour version would be even funnier, but more poignant, and again would be of special interest to viewers in the North East.

Written by Whitley Bay-born Ian La Frenais and his sidekick Dick Clement and set in Newcastle, the rebooted series followed the scrapes of an older Terry and Bob and their often hilarious, but sometimes uncomfortable passage through the rapidly changing world of the 1970s.

The writing pair - who would later pen the likes of Porridge and Auf Wiedersehen, Pet - would not only strike comedy gold, but throw an illuminating light on the shifting times.

If the resolutely blue-collared Terry harked back to the old world of betting shops and corner-end boozers, Bob and his bossy new wife, Thelma, aspired to the upwardly mobile new world of badminton clubs and fondue parties.

Terry lived with his mother in an old terraced house. Bob and Thelma, superbly played by Brigit Forsyth, lived in the newly-built Elm Lodge Housing Estate (which in reality was Highfields Estate in Killingworth). Their tidy semi-detached house was done out in fashionably period orange and brown, with all mod cons.

A full six years before the election of Conservative Prime Minister Margaret Thatcher would usher in radical changes to attitudes and life in Britain, La Frenais and Clement had their fingers on the pulse of a changing nation.

The show's memorable opening and closing theme song dripped with nostalgia. Alongside images of Newcastle under transformation ran the lines: "Oh what happened to you, whatever happened to me? What became of the people we used to be?"

Terry looked back to the 1960s. Bob looked ahead to the rest of the 1970s. It was brilliantly perceptive - and prophetic. Britain was changing.

A traffic jam on Newcastle's Swan House roundabout, June 1979. The decade saw areas of Newcastle transformed

The 1970s began with the last knockings of Harold Wilson's Labour government and ended with a Tory, and Britain's first woman Prime Minister Margaret Thatcher resident in 10, Downing Street.

The decade is often portrayed as one of economic strife and political instability in the UK. There were strikes, power cuts and governments pitched against trade unions.

With the folk of Britain getting to grips with decimal currency, and the Northern Ireland 'troubles' in the headlines, it was inflation that became the major economic challenge.

Unemployment was relatively low, but the price of petrol and the everyday cost of living would begin to rocket.

If housewives grumbled about the rising price of baked beans at the supermarket, house prices - especially - went through the roof. In 1971, an average UK house cost £5,500. A year later the price had soared to around £7,800.

In the North East, the decade began with the traditional heavy industries - coalmining, shipbuilding and engineering - still present, if not all correct. By the end of the 1970s, a period of steep industrial decline was under way as cheap foreign competition and increasingly outdated working practices began to take their toll.

The workplace became an arena of conflict between unions and management. As early in the decade as January 12, 1971, the Newcastle Evening Chronicle was reporting: "Tyneside shipyards came to an almost complete standstill as more than 4,000 workers walked out at lunchtime in protest at the Industrial Relations Bill.

"The strike hit Swan Hunter production at Hebburn, South Shields, and the Cleland yard near Wallsend, while there were brief walk-outs up and down the Tyne at other locations."

It was the type of story that would be reported up and down the country over the coming years.

As the mid-1970s arrived, rising oil prices and industrial action saw the lights go out – literally - across Britain, and Ted Heath's Tory government in crisis.

Labour under the returning Harold Wilson and then James Callaghan inherited the mess, battled in vain against inflation, only to be replaced by Margaret Thatcher.

In Newcastle, the decade would see the cityscape undergo profound changes.

In a process begun in the 1960s by council leader T. Dan Smith, much that was 'old' was swept away to be replaced by the 'new'.

In Newcastle's East and West Ends, Victorian-built terraced streets that provided homes for generations of workers were demolished. The strikingly designed Byker Wall housing complex emerged in the early 1970s.

The multi-storey Swan House and Westgate House office blocks were intended as new 'gateways' to a modern, forward-thinking city that was turning its back on post-war gloom.

The Central Motorway, opened in 1973, would carve a route through the middle of Newcastle as the number of cars on the road soared.

Across the city, two thirds of the Georgian-built, Palladium-style Eldon Square was demolished to make way for an eponymous giant shopping complex opened in 1976.

In the middle years of the decade, it was impossible for shoppers and motorists to escape major building work at the Haymarket, Central Station and Grey's Monument areas of the city. Building work on the new Tyne and Wear Metro system began in 1974. Underground stations were constructed and tunnels were driven underneath the streets in advance of its opening in August 1980. The Metro would revolutionise public transport in the region.

Away from more weighty matters, however, day-to-day life in the 1970s was also characterised by memorable pop music, TV shows, films and sporting action.

For those of us who grew up during the decade, it was often great fun.

Our parents were generally better off than their parents had been, so while we'd play endless street games or roamed happily with friends in the '70s sunshine, we lived in houses that had colour televisions, stereo record players, and even early computer games.

Meanwhile, parked outside, and unlike a decade earlier, there would likely be a family car – maybe a Vauxhall Viva, a Morris 1100, or a Ford Cortina to take us on weekend trips out.

And we'd eagerly chomp on the likes of Tudor Crisps - which were manufactured in Newcastle - Curly Wurlies and Amazin' Raisin Bars, bought with more pocket money than children 10 or 20 years earlier had received.

In music, the decade spawned a range of styles - pop, rock, glam, disco, punk and more.

Most of the world's major acts stopped off on their tours at Newcastle City Hall, or the Mayfair Ballroom.

David Bowie, Elton John, the Rolling Stones, The Who, Led Zeppelin and Pink Floyd were just some of the A-list rockers who came to town. And there was mayhem at the City Hall when the teenybopper boy band Bay City Rollers appeared in 1975.

Each summer, the Hoppings – Europe's biggest travelling funfair – set up stall on the Town Moor for a week. Tens of thousands flocked there – and still do; and thousands more enjoyed the now-discontinued Tyneside Summer Exhibition.

On TV, we kids might enjoy watching Dads' Army, the Goodies, or Blue Peter, but a trip to 'the pictures' was still a treat.

Thousands greeted the Queen and Prince Philip at Newcastle's recently opened Eldon Square shopping centre, July 1977

Actor Michael Caine on Westgate Road, Newcastle, taking time out from filming Get Carter, July 1970

We might go to see Jaws at Westgate Road's ABC in 1975, or Star Wars at The Odeon two years later, or Grease at the 'Haymarket' in 1978 – all cinemas which are sadly no more.

Come 1977, while Elvis Presley permanently left the building on the other side of the Atlantic, the Queen celebrated her Silver Jubilee with a nationwide tour which took in Tyneside, Wearside and Teesside.

In the same year, there were also the most unlikely of visits to the region in the shape of American President Jimmy Carter and world heavyweight boxing champion Muhammad Ali.

For football fans on Tyneside, the decade began with the Inter City Fairs Cup gleaming in the St James' Park trophy cabinet. Against the odds and in their first ever European campaign, Newcastle United lifted the trophy that was the forerunner of the UEFA Cup and today's Europa League.

United fans fell in love at once with continental football and huge crowds flocked to midweek evening games at Gallowgate.

First, Feyenoord of Holland, then Sporting Lisbon, Real Zaragoza, Vitoria Setubal. Glasgow Rangers and finally Ujpest Dozsa were each dispensed over two legs during United's glorious march to the trophy, which culminated on June 11, 1969 on a balmy night in Budapest.

Later, the 1970s Toon Army would thrill to the exploits of London-born goal machine Malcolm Macdonald. Twenty-one-year-old Supermac fired in 30 goals in

his first season and was promptly called into Sir Alf Ramsey's England squad.

Sadly, the Magpies could not follow up their Fairs Cup success and, in the years that followed, lost the 1974 FA Cup final to Liverpool, and the League Cup final two years later to Manchester City. A period of steep decline followed.

As 1979 turned into 1980, Newcastle United found themselves in the oblivion of English football's Second Division.

In the wider world, the new decade that was the 1980s would deliver its own set of very real challenges and problems for the North East – but that's another story.

For now, enjoy our photographs of Newcastle and Tyneside in the 1970s.

The images come from the fantastic archive of the Newcastle Chronicle and Journal, and the Daily Mirror.

The majority capture the life and times of Newcastle during the decade, and there are others showing wider Tyneside.

Along with the text, they give a taste of what it was like to live in the region during that unique period.

Dave Morton, July 2018

1970

A striking image of Newcastle on the cusp of change. We're looking at Clara Street, Benwell, in September, 1970. The two ladies are unnamed, and we can see that some of the houses are derelict, while others are still occupied. In the distance, on the other side of the River Tyne, sits Dunston Power Station with its landmark giant chimneys.

This was a time when large areas of old housing here in the city's West End, and elsewhere, had fallen into terminal decline and were facing imminent demolition. Clearance of the long parallel terraces, such as Clara Street, which ran down to the Tyne began during the 1960s and into the '70s. Meanwhile, Dunston Power Station – firstly A station, then its replacement B station – stood between 1910 and the mid-1980s. The shopping temple that is the Metrocentre – opened in 1986 – stands in its place today.

Skinhead gangs emerged from Britain's inner cities in the late 1960s and early 1970s. Fans of reggae music, their dress code involved 'half-mast' trousers and Dr Marten boots. The sight of a gang of shaven-headed lads wearing immaculately polished cherry red or shiny black 'Docs' was enough to make the average law-abiding citizen quickly stride off in the opposite direction.

This group of likely lads – and lasses – had just been evicted from Whitley Bay's Spanish City fairground for unruly behaviour on May 31, 1970. They will all be well into their 60s today!

A winter's evening view of Marks & Spencer on Northumberland Street, Newcastle in December, 1970. It is one of the North East's most popular retail stores. Opened in September 1932, this was also the year Newcastle United beat Arsenal to win the FA Cup, Sydney Harbour Bridge opened, and a new house would cost you £540.

This wasn't the city's first M&S. A much humbler affair, the original Penny Bazaar in the city's Grainger Market, had opened in 1895. It still sells goods to this day and is an old Geordie 'curiosity' which is worth a visit. As for the new store on Northumberland Street, it would become a North East shopping institution.

As the go-to place to buy undies, M&S had unveiled its first women's bra in 1926. During the war years, the 1941 'Making of Civilian Clothing (Restriction Orders)' meant the company could use only five buttons, two pockets and four metres of stitching for every item of clothing it made. The 1950s saw glamour come bouncing back with the introduction of the Christian Dior-influenced New Style for some of its women's clothing.

Into the 1960s, new technology saw chilled - rather than frozen - chickens go on sale for the first time. And if you shopped at M&S during the 1970s, frozen pizzas went on sale in 1972, and curries and Chinese dishes were launched - unsuccessfully at first - in 1974. Later, the 1980s saw boil-in-the-bag and microwave meals first become available.

As for the Newcastle store thousands of us use every day, it's undergone many changes and improvements since it opened on September 16, 1932. Between 1936 and 1951, it was extended several times. And throughout the 1960s, the store was extended again over four stages, growing to 71,500 sq ft. On June 24, 1963, a self-contained food section was introduced with direct access from Prudhoe Street.

By 1996, the store became the second largest M&S store in the country after Marble Arch, following the completion of a major redevelopment programme, increasing the sales floor from 72,000 sq ft to 140,000 sq ft, including a new customer restaurant with 300 seats.

Everybody out! Strikes were a common feature of the industrial landscape of 1970s Britain, and these female workers at Reyrolle in Hebburn downed tools in 1970.

Frenchman Alphonse Reyrolle founded his giant electrical switchgear company in the town in 1901. At its peak, Reyrolle employed 12,000 people and manufactured switchgear for power stations worldwide. Production was halted briefly in 1926 when news reached the girls in the workforce that silver screen idol Rudolph Valentino had died, and mass hysteria followed for a short time!

Reyrolle would go on to merge with other electronics companies, but work at the Hebburn site finally came to an end in 2010.

Bainbridge was one of Newcastle's favourite department stores for decade upon decade. Here we see it at its original Market Street location as the autumn dusk settles on October 10, 1970.

Its story began way back in the second year of Queen Victoria's reign, 1838, when it was founded by Emerson Muschamp Bainbridge. Enjoying growth and popularity as the years passed, on Monday, February 2, 1953, Bainbridge became a branch of the John Lewis Partnership. In October 1976, there was a major relocation from Market Street to the newly-built Eldon Square shopping centre where the shop still trades today.

Although heavier merchandise was moved by van, staff pushed supermarket trolleys or carried lighter stock in plastic bins or by hand.

In 2002 the Bainbridge name was changed to John Lewis Newcastle, and by 2014 over 600 so-called partners worked there.

John Lewis remains one of the North East's most important and historic retailers.

Under the floodlights of St James' Park, on Wednesday, September 30, 1970, one of Newcastle United's most famous and dramatic post-war games took place.

If memories of Barcelona in 1997 and Juventus in 2002 are fresher and more vivid, the 2-0 humbling of Italian giants Inter Milan is up there with those latter-day classics.

Having won the Inter Cities Fairs Cup (the predecessor of the UEFA Cup and Europa League) at their first attempt and as rank outsiders in 1969, this was the third season in a row United rubbed shoulders with the elite of European football.

When the draw for the first round of the 1970-71 tournament was made, again the Magpies weren't given a chance. Inter were one of the biggest clubs in world football, having lifted the Serie A title ten times and, indeed, they would go on to be Italian champions again at the end of this campaign. Meanwhile, several of Inter's stars - Facchetti, Burgnich, Mazzola and Boninsegna - had played for Italy in the 1970 World Cup in Mexico, succumbing only in the final to Pele's brilliant Brazil team.

In the first leg at the San Siro, United played well, earning a 1-1 draw. A Wyn Davies goal was only cancelled out in the dying stages of the game.

A week later, 56,495 turned out at Gallowgate for what would be a night of drama under the giant floodlight pylons. United, wearing all red and with their famously vociferous crowd behind them, attacked from the start. In the 29th minute, captain Bobby Moncur rose unchallenged to meet Pop Robson's corner and his firm header gave the Magpies a 1-0 lead.

With St James' in meltdown, the Italians soon lost their heads and a clash between Italian goalkeeper, Vieri, and Davies led to an almighty brawl. The five-minute bust-up culminated with Vieri punching the referee and police officers entering the field of play to end the melee. With the keeper promptly sent off and the crowd in full voice, the Magpies with their tails up continued to besiege the visitors, hitting the bar three times before Davies popped up to nod in the rebound after 70 minutes.

It would be 32 years before Inter Milan graced St James' Park again, but the visiting stars of 2002 - Christian Vieri, Hernan Crespo and co - were a different proposition, crushing United 4-1 in the Champions' League.

Film-goers queue to see Carry On Loving at the Odeon Cinema, on Pilgrim Street, Newcastle, on December 8, 1970. When this photo was taken, the golden age of the silver screen was well in the past, and cinemas across the region were beginning to struggle in the face of the unstoppable rise of television.

For those movie-goers who did go to see the on-screen antics of Sid James, Kenneth Williams and co in 1970, there was the added attraction of the cinema's Northumbrian restaurant which dished up a mean mixed grill and was one of the city's favourite eating places.

The venue started life as The Paramount back in 1931 – a state-of-the-art picture palace which seated 2,602 people. A report from the opening night described it as a "cathedral of motion pictures". In 1939 the Paramount was bought out by the Odeon chain and continued to pull in the punters over the decades.

From the 1960s, however, audiences slowly declined as people's leisure time tastes changed. By the close of the millennium and with the rise of the competing multiplex cinema experience, home computer games, and multi-channel TV, Newcastle Odeon had had its day.

In November 2002 the final credits rolled, and The Odeon relocated to The Gate on Newgate Street, before becoming the Empire and ending The Odeon's long association with the city. The building was left to decay and, despite opposition, was demolished in 2016 to make way for a new retail quarter.

An atmospheric shot of Lloyds Bank on Newcastle's Grey Street on December 8, 1970. Designed by John Dobson in 1839, the building is still home to the "black horse" bank today. Lloyds moved in here in 1908 but the site already had a long history, having been home to a Victorian bank called Lambton and Co. Much earlier, a 13th century monastery stood here, then a grand house called Anderson Place where King Charles I was held as an open prisoner by the Scots, in 1646, during the English Civil War.

The late 1960s and early '70s saw radical changes to Gateshead's town centre. The busy High Street had long been the main route into Newcastle. But this was a time when many of the High Street's pubs and cinemas were demolished to make way for new junctions and a flyover – seen under construction in 1970 – that would now take traffic to and from Newcastle. Businesses and shops on the street would come to struggle in the years that followed.

A bleak view of Gateshead East railway station on a rain-lashed January 14, 1970. The station had opened on August 30, 1859, and sat on the southern end of the recently-opened High Level Bridge. It served generations of train passengers travelling to South Shields and Sunderland before closing on November 23, 1981 - a week after the new Metro line to Heworth opened. Gateshead East remained substantially intact until it was damaged by fire in the late 1980s, and by 1990 the platforms and the track-level buildings had been demolished. Gateshead now has the dubious distinction of being one of the largest towns not to have a station on the national rail network.

The classic film Get Carter was under production on Tyneside in 1970. We see star of the movie, Michael Caine, and fellow actors, George Sewell and Ian Hendry, at Wallsend on October 1. Released in March the following year, Get Carter tells the violent tale of London gangster, Jack Carter, played by Caine, who returns to his home city, Newcastle, to avenge the death of his brother.

With a budget of £750,000, the movie was shot in the North East and used the people and places of the region as a dramatic backdrop to the action.

If it received mixed reviews and made just moderate money at the box office in 1971, in more recent years it has been critically acclaimed in its own right, and as an influence on latter day classics The Long Good Friday and Lock, Stock and Two Smoking Barrels.

The film footage captures the region at a unique time in its history, depicting a long-vanished vision of Tyneside. The skies are slate grey, the wind howls, pubs are filled with brawling drinkers and cigarette smokers, while guest houses have bed pans underneath the stained mattresses.

Director Mike Hodges said: "The visual drama took my breath away. Seeing the great bridges crossing the Tyne, the waterfront, the terraced houses steeped up each side of the deep valley… We'd got there in time. But only just."

The dramatic landscape would soon be swept away by 1970s urban re-development.

Get Carter remains not only a great film, but a time capsule showing old Tyneside on the brink of profound physical change.

Juvenile jazz bands were all the rage on Tyneside during the decade and, in 1970, North Shields and Tynemouth Grenadiers paid a visit to historic Tynemouth Priory.

The story of Tynemouth, however, began many centuries earlier. The headland towering over the mouth of the Tyne has been settled since the Iron Age. The Romans occupied it then, in the 7th century, a monastery was built there and later fortified. The ancient monastery on the site was sacked twice by the Danes and rebuilt each time.

Three ancient kings are said to have been buried there and later, in medieval times, it became a safe haven for a string of English kings and their queens in politically unstable times.

A village and port sprung up in the shadow of the monastery, sparking a centuries-long dispute with powerful Newcastle over shipping rights.

Much later, the arrival of the railway from Newcastle in the late 19th century saw the emergence of Tynemouth - much like near-by Whitley Bay - as a newfangled tourist destination.

Tynemouth Station opened in 1882 on a new mainline, paving the way for thousands of holiday-makers who flocked to the beaches. Today it's a Metro station and its ornate Victorian ironwork canopies have earned it Grade II listed status.

The wide expanse of the Blue Flag-rated Longsands has been a draw for visitors for well over a century.

The construction of Tynemouth pier began in 1854 and took over 40 years to complete. In 1898 the original curved design proved inadequate against a huge storm and the centre section was washed away. The pier was rebuilt in a straighter line and completed in 1909.

The Collingwood Monument is the impressive memorial to Lord Collingwood, Nelson's second-in-command at Trafalgar, who led the Royal Navy to victory after Nelson was killed.

Tyneside's striking banana-yellow buses were out in force amid heavy traffic in Grainger Street, Newcastle on July 14, 1970. The street was named after the 19th century builder Richard Grainger who created the Newcastle city centre we know and love today. Working alongside the brilliant architect John Dobson, it has been written of Grainger that he "found Newcastle of bricks and timber and left it in stone".

(Top) In 1970, the River Tyne in its old industrial heartland was a very different place. Certainly at Wallsend, the traditional staple of North East working life, shipbuilding, was still in full swing - even if the industry faced growing challenges.

Today, the Tyne is quieter but these striking images - taken on November 19, 1970 - show towering cranes and a hubbub of activity around a giant vessel under construction. The 250,000-ton supertanker Esso Hibernia being fitted out at Swan Hunter, Wallsend.

The Hibernia was the sister ship of the better-known Esso Northumbria, and one of a series of supertankers constructed at the yard in the late 1960s and early '70s. We see workers crawling all over the tanker, getting the vessel ship-shape and ready for sea trials.

The giant oil tanker had been launched in April 1970, when a section of the opposite bank of the Tyne at Hebburn needed to be excavated to allow for the ship speeding down the slipway in to the river. Apparently the director responsible for the calculation of the launch got a drenching when the resulting wash produced a wave which swept up the far shore.

As for the vessel itself, the Chronicle reported at the time: "The overall impression is one of sheer scale.

"She is just a long, gigantic steel box - a quarter-of-a-mile long, 60 yards wide and 30 yards deep - with an eight-storey block of flats in the end."

But for Captain John Phillips and the 31-man crew, living conditions weren't too shabby at all. The Chronicle declared: "Away from the functional, the Hibernia is a world of tiled floors and polished wooden surfaces. A world of bedside lamps and pictures on the walls; officers' suites with two settees and plenty of armchairs; and lounges with cocktail bars and televisions."

The Hibernia's sea-going life extended to April 1983, when she was scrapped in the Taiwanese port city of Kaohsiung.

(Bottom) The Gun Hotel, as photographed on October 7, 1970, was one of a host of pubs along Newcastle's famous Scotswood Road. The most notable was probably the Robin Adair, which gets a mention in that Geordie Anthem, the Blaydon Races.

Since 1850, it is reckoned at least 46 pubs – maybe more – have come and gone on Scotswood Road. But there are thought to have been only four pubs which sat squarely on to Scotswood Road. The others were on street corners leading on to the main road.

Today, nearly all of them are gone apart from a handful on the St James' Boulevard and Marlborough Crescent section of the road.

Derwent Tower, or the 'Dunston Rocket' as it was aptly nicknamed, loomed over Tyneside for 40 years. We see it here under construction in 1970.

Designed and built in the 'brutalist' architectural style of the day, building work on Derwent Tower began in 1968, and the project was complete by 1971. Yet only four decades later it would be razed to the ground.

The 280-ft, 29-storey building would be the tallest on Tyneside and, with living space for 1,300 people, was hailed as the solution to the lack of low-cost housing.

The brains behind the Dunston Rocket, London-based architect Owen Luder, was also responsible for the equally controversial Trinity Square car park in Gateshead town centre.

Right from the off, the Dunston structure divided opinion. Some residents described it as a "hellhole", while others liked living there.

The Rocket also had a starring role in a Tudor Crisps television advert in the 1970s, in which a paperboy manages to bribe his mate to deliver newspapers to the top floor of the giant tower. "Tudor Crisps? I'd climb a mountain!"

After years of bad press and controversy, the last resident moved out in 2007, and in September 2012, Derwent Tower was demolished.

A bird's eye view of Redheugh Park, the home of Gateshead FC in 1970. It was the club's home from its formation in 1930 until 1971 when the ground was bulldozed. Gateshead played in the football league until 1960 when they controversially failed to gain re-election. The club, who today play their home games at Gateshead International Stadium, agonisingly missed out on a return to the Football League in 2014 when they lost to Cambridge in the Skrill play-off final at Wembley

Dockers at the Albert Edward Dock in North Shields suspend a strike in 1970 to unload a massive cargo of fish from the Ranger Ajax, a freezer trawler. The ship had arrived at North Shields after a 10-week Arctic trip with her refrigeration system out of action.

1971

An atmospheric view of the bottom of Newcastle's Pudding Chare in November 1971. The old lane linking the city's Bigg Market and Collingwood Street/Westgate Road, is one of the earliest recorded streets in Newcastle.

The term "chare" is a North Eastern word for a narrow, winding lane. Newcastle had, and still has, a number of these old chares, although many of them, such as Grinding Chare, Pallister's Chare and Peppercorn Chare, were demolished after the devastating Great Fire of Newcastle in 1854.

In 1827, Pudding Chare was described as leading "to the Bigg Market, but is narrow, dirty, and inconvenient for carriages". By the early years of Queen Victoria's reign, the lane hosted pubs, now long-gone, including the Friendly Sons of Erin, the Hatter's Arms, the Salutation Inn, the Rose Inn, the Collingwood Inn, and the Wellington Hotel, which today is the site of a popular bar, Revolution, having been converted from a grand 20th century branch of Barclays Bank.

Looking further back, the first written record of the lane appears in 1333, and there are subsequent mentions, including Puddyngchare (1447), and Puddingchaire (1572) as the centuries pass.

There are several theories behind the origins of Pudding Chare's unusual name. It could be a reference to black pudding which was sold in the nearby Flesh Market - later Cloth Market. It could be a reference to the hidden stream of High or Pow Dene - or to the intestine-like winding lane. Alternatively, it is thought, 'pudding' could merely be a description of the surface of what would have been little more than a muddy lane.

Youngsters in Newcastle's West End take to the streets in 1971 demanding the reopening of the popular Snow Street swimming baths in Arthurs Hill.

Newcastle's main retail thoroughfare, Northumberland Street, was packed with shoppers in the run-up to Christmas, 1971. Once-popular stores Woolworth and Littlewoods are long-gone, but Fenwick and Marks and Spencer remain.

In the early 18th century, long before the shoppers arrived, it was described as a "very well-built street, having in it some very pretty houses standing in the middle of gardens and shady fields". In 1827, it was reported as having "a most airy, light, and elegant appearance". But later it was described as a row of old brick houses that "are rapidly becoming shops".

For decades, traffic passed up and down Northumberland Street. Indeed, it was part of the main A1 London-Edinburgh route until the building of the city by-pass in the early 1970s.

One of the most memorable games witnessed at St James' Park saw Malcolm Macdonald score a hat trick against Liverpool in his home debut for Newcastle United.

United won the thrilling game 3-2 and it was the start of a five-year spell when the prolific striker became an idol on Tyneside.

Here we see Supermac and his midfield teammate Terry Hibbitt celebrate one of the three goals.

It was Saturday, August 21, 1971, a near-40,000 Gallowgate crowd got their first sighting of the Toon's 21-year-old record £180,000 signing from Luton Town - and he did not disappoint. With Kevin Keegan (who would later become a hero himself at Newcastle United) and Emlyn Hughes netting for the Reds, it was left to the speedy, bustling Macdonald to claim victory for United.

And on a highly memorable day, he would finally be carried off injured after a clash with visiting goalkeeper Ray Clemence late in the match.

Years later, Supermac recalled: "I remember that even very early on in my Newcastle career, we played some really neat, cute stuff.

"If you watch the footage of that game today, you can see the interplay between myself and the likes of Terry Hibbitt and John Tudor. There was an understanding there straight away.

"The game was the stuff of dreams really, and I scored a hat-trick. The pick of the goals was the second one at the Gallowgate End where I turned on the edge of the 18-yard box and just buried it.

"The Geordie public knew straight away what I was all about. After the third goal, the cheering turned into a crowd chant: 'Supermac, superstar, how many goals have you scored so far?'

"The chant was adapted from that famous song in the musical Jesus Christ Superstar, of course - and it was almost as if the crowd had been given song sheets. An amazing day."

Winter snow had come early to Gateshead, on November 23, 1971. The Morris Minors and Austin Minis are struggling up and down a slushy Bensham Road.

More than four decades later, the cafe on the left has become a general dealer's store, the old shops and flats on the right have given way to modern housing, while St Cuthbert's Church at the bottom remains.

Designed by eminent Tyneside architect John Dobson and built between 1846 and 1848, it occupies a prominent position on Bensham bank, with fine views down to the River Tyne - and beyond. The last service took place there in 1991.

Today, Bensham remains a busy suburb for families who work in and around Tyneside - and it houses a community of around 5,000 Orthodox Jews whose ancestors flocked to the area in the last quarter of the 19th century.

Then, during the Nazi era, Jewish businessmen - refugees from Hitler's Germany - settled in Gateshead, making it one of the largest orthodox Jewish centres outside the US and Israel. Some of the shops on bustling Coatsworth Road used to - and presumably still do - sell the very best bagels!

It's March 11, 1971, and Newcastle Civic Centre has four new receptionists, looking smart in their uniforms.

Officially opened in 1968 by King Olav of Norway, the Civic Centre was a long time in the making. Plans for a new 'town hall' dated back to before World War II, but it wasn't until November 1960 that the city's Lord Mayor laid the foundation stone.

The building work was completed by 1967 for a total outlay of £4,855,000. As a seat of government it replaced Newcastle's Victorian-built Town Hall in the Bigg Market, which had fallen into disrepair and was finally demolished in 1973. Today the Civic Centre is considered to be a classic of its time and is Grade II-listed.

Over the last five decades it has been the focal point for official visits to the city by passing royals, and even American presidents. Famously in 1977, US president Jimmy Carter stood in front of a crowd of thousands of Geordies, before announcing, in that famous Georgian drawl: "Howay the Lads."

It has also been a meeting point for public demonstrations - all part of the city's and nation's democratic freedoms.

Unlike many other 1960s buildings that have come and gone, Newcastle's Civic Centre remains one of the most striking on Tyneside. Features such as the distinctive tower with its seahorses, the River God Tyne statue, and the murals by Victor Passmore mean it is so much more than a concrete tower block.

Two girls – possibly even twin sisters – enjoying one of the rides at Newcastle's annual Hoppings funfair on the Town Moor, June 20, 1971.

Fenwick – or Fenwick's as most local people call it – has been one of Newcastle's favourite stores for generations. Here we see its Food Hall in February 1971.

The store on Northumberland Street is renowned for its quality goods and services. From the annual Christmas window - which began in 1971 - to the restaurants and cafes, to the top-of-the-range household goods, to the huge array of high fashion on sale, and to the richly-stocked Food Hall, the store has been cited as Newcastle's own version of Harrod's.

It was mantle-maker and furrier John James Fenwick who opened the first humble shop at 5 Northumberland Street in March, 1885. It's hard to imagine today, but the retail giant started life as a single house snapped up by the young shop assistant for the sum of £181.

The fledgling business initially sold mantles, silk goods, dresses, fabrics and trimming, but expansion was rapid and Fenwick and his son, Fred, soon bought up adjoining Northumberland Street properties, numbers 37 and 38 - and later number 40. These formed the shop frontage still used by Fenwick in 2017.

Back in Victorian England, Fenwick's next acquisition was a store in Bond Street, London, opened in 1891, and today one of Britain's leading retail temples.

It was Fred's visit to Paris, however, which led to a shopping revolution. At Bon Marche, he witnessed a ground-breaking form of retail trading, a department store, where a variety of goods and services was sold under one roof, as opposed to separate shops. That principle was applied in Newcastle and London, and Fenwick has never looked back.

Today, the famous brand has stores in Brent Cross, Bracknell, York, Canterbury, Tunbridge Wells, Kingston, and Colchester as well as Bond Street and Newcastle.

A classic Tyneside view, relatively unchanged over the last century – this is Dean Street in Newcastle in October, 1971. The street's dramatic descent stems from the ancient geography of the city, and generations of folk will have tackled the steep gradient - up and down to the Quayside.

The building on the corner of Side and Dean Street is Milburn House which today boasts state-of-the-art office space in a Grade-II listed building. The office block was built in 1905, with finance from the wealthy local Milburn family.

Because of the family's connection with shipping, the building was designed like an ocean-going liner, with the floors labelled deck-style - A at the top and G on the ground floor.

In its early days almost 1,000 people worked there.

Today, the smart street with its restaurants and specialist shops reveals little of the area's history.

Dean Steet was built over a stream called the Lort Burn, which ran down to the Tyne and was basically an open sewer. Meat waste from the old Flesh Market was also thrown into the burn providing, surely, a rich aroma in the area. In 1827 it was described as a "vast nauseous hollow, equally unhealthy and inconvenient".

Next time you're heading down Dean Street for a pint or a pizza, maybe remember that!

An image which sums up the wholesale demolition work going on in Newcastle's East and West Ends in the late 1960s and early 1970s. Here we see a shattered and abandoned street in the Scotswood Road area of Elswick in 1971.

It was a time of the mass demolition of houses, shops and pubs which had stood for over a century. This was an era of major change in the city as the concept of "progress" was busily sweeping away great swathes of the old. In place of these former homes, new houses and looming tower blocks had been thrown up.

The process had begun in the 1960s as part of Newcastle Council Leader T Dan Smith's vision of "a city in the sky".

These "slum" clearances may have torn down housing that was not fit for purpose, but it also dispersed deeply entrenched communities.

More than four decades later, for many people there remains a deep nostalgia for the vanished life and times of Newcastle's old West End where the streets, pubs and shops teemed with life.

A long-standing Newcastle pub, this is Bourgogne's in Newgate Street on October 23, 1971. It had been known as the Mason's Arms until around 1876 when it was bought by a firm of French winemakers called Bourgogne. Standing opposite St Andrew's Church, and pronounced as "Burgoynes" by local people, the favourite watering hole would be demolished in 1972 - like a whole swathe of the city's old buildings – as the new Eldon Square shopping centre was constructed. A new Bourgogne's, lacking the charm and history of the original, was opened in later years.

Traffic heading into Gateshead, from Newcastle across the Tyne Bridge - with the Dun Cow pub on the right, marooned in the middle of a sea of traffic, and now closed for many years - on June 8, 1971.

There had been an inn here, possibly dating back to the 17th century, before the last version of the pub - once known as the Red Cow - was built in 1939.

Newcastle City Hall, across the decades, has played host to some of the biggest music stars of all time. The early 1970s, especially, saw rock royalty making appearances at the venue on a routine basis.

Pink Floyd, The Who, Led Zeppelin, Rod Stewart, David Bowie, Elton John, and many more, regularly graced the City Hall stage in an era when rock music was at its zenith.

The Beatles, of course, played the venue several times in the early 1960s, but by 1971 there was arguably no more famous band on the planet than the Rolling Stones. On March 4 of that year, the iconic venue on Northumberland Road played host to the Stones for the opening date - and indeed a second show on the same night – of their first British tour since 1967. That was the year Mick Jagger, Keith Richards and the boys disappeared to tax havens in Southern Europe.

Fast forward to 1971, and Chronicle photographers were on hand to capture the arrival by train of the band and their wives and girlfriends at Newcastle Central Station. They were also snapped paparazzi-style, as our photograph shows, at Gateshead's Five Bridges hotel – later the Swallow Hotel - one of the plushest on Tyneside at the time. And finally, they were captured in action live on stage at the City Hall.

Tickets for the shows were 75p in the newly Decimalised UK - or 15 shillings in old money. Support was provided by that great British blues band, The Groundhogs.

Meanwhile, a slightly new-look Stones hit the stage, featuring fresh-faced Mick Taylor on guitar (replacing the late Brian Jones), plus a two-piece brass section, and Nicky Hopkins on piano. Punters at the show, we reported, remained reserved but appreciative throughout, with the Stones delivering effective renditions of Jumping Jack Flash, Honky Tonk Women, Brown Sugar, Satisfaction, Street Fighting Man, and more.

Twenty-eight-year-old Jagger was resplendent in pink satin suit, while his cohort, Richards, also 28, churned out the classic riffs on a see-through perspex guitar.

At a time when the biggest rock acts played in the provinces, the tour rolled on to the likes of Coventry, Brighton and Leeds before winding up in London.

As for the Newcastle date, a review in the Guardian declared: "If it does nothing else, this tour should reassert their extraordinary talents as showmen, and remind the public of their great contribution to British rock. Above all the Stones still mean excitement and fun."

For the Rolling Stones, it was yet another memorable encounter with a Newcastle audience in a musical relationship which dated back to the Club A'Gogo in the early 1960s, and would see them return - to St James' Park – in 1982, and again in 1990.

The 1970s – a decade when beauty contests were all the rage. A Miss Tyne Tees Television contest was held at Tynemouth Open Air Swimming Pool on July 24, 1971. The winner, Lynne Charlton, was crowned by Tyne Tees' Rod Griffiths. The runners-up were Sheila Mitchell and Pamela Graham.

Tynemouth Outdoor Pool had opened at Sharpness Point in the sweltering summer of 1925. There had been calls to build a pool here since around 1905 after several people drowned swimming in the unpredictable North Sea. Once built, the pool was automatically filled by the incoming tide and was, for decades, a popular venue for local families and holidaymakers. It would host regular swimming galas and competitions, and was a magnet for thousands.

Terraces were designed to hold up to 2,000 people, while visitors could hire tents to use as changing rooms – and retain their modesty.

Sadly, with the rise of foreign holidays, the opening of a nearby indoor pool, fewer outdoor bathers, and the mounting cost of cleaning and repairs, the open-air pool was finally closed in the mid-90s.

In 1996 the council made a botched effort to revamp the pool with the intention of converting it into a 'rock pool' by scattering it with large stones and boulders. The neglect continued, however, and what had been a fine outdoor lido soon became a controversial eyesore.

At the time of writing, a group called Friends of Tynemouth Outdoor Pool was working to revive the run-down site.

Crowds flocked to the beach at Tynemouth on a roasting hot day in July 1971. For anyone who had a transistor radio with them that day, there's a good chance they'd have heard Chirpy Chirpy Cheep Cheep by Middle Of The Road which was number one in the pop charts at the time!

A view of the Tyne Bridge, from Newcastle looking into Gateshead in September, 1971. The world-famous symbol of Tyneside was officially opened by King George V and Queen Mary on Wednesday, October 10, 1928, arriving in a horse-drawn Ascot Landau carriage from Jesmond railway station. Thousands had lined the route from 8am. When the king finally declared the bridge open, the Evening Chronicle reported how it prompted "shrill whistles from ships, workshops and factories, and the full-bodied hooting of steamer sirens. Bells clamoured from church towers, an aeroplane flew low, and bands played."

It's September 30, 1971, and ladies from the East End of Newcastle enjoy a laugh at the last remaining corporation washhouse on Shipley Street, Byker. This was the last time residents would use the old facilities at a time more and more family homes were acquiring washing machines.

1972

A stunning image from a vanished industrial Tyneside. The tanker, World Unicorn, takes shape at Wallsend's Swan Hunter shipyard toward the end of 1972. In the terraced street, children play in the shadow of the giant ship.

Years later, the girl skipping in the photograph contacted the Newcastle Evening Chronicle when it was published in the newspaper.

She said: "I was called Angela Anderson then, and I would have been 12 or 13.

"We got used to ships being built at the end of our street, which was Hunter Street, Wallsend. It was just a way of life.

"The noise of the men working on the ships, the buzzers, and the workers piling out after their shifts were just part of day-to-day living.

"We used to watch the ships being launched from an attic in my friend's house at the bottom of the street.

"My father, Joseph, was the driver of the crane you can see on the picture - and he would take his binoculars up into the cabin to keep an eye on me, in case I got up to any mischief. It was fun growing up there."

The streets of houses backing on to the shipyard would be bulldozed a couple of years later. The houses stood where the Roman museum, Segedunum, stands today.

The World Unicorn would be launched in May 1973 by Princess Anne, before ending its days at the breakers' yard in Kaohsiung, Taiwan in 1984.

This fine view of two of Newcastle's most notable locations – the Central Station and Castle Keep – was captured on May 25, 1972.

The Castle Keep – the city's oldest building - and its 13th century gatehouse the Black Gate, were once part of a much larger fortress. Given its tumultuous history, it is miraculous that so much of Newcastle's castle has survived intact.

The site has been used for defensive purposes since Roman times. The name of the original fort, Pons Aelius, referred to the Roman name for bridge – pons - and the Emperor Hadrian whose family name was Aelius.

The 'New Castle' which gave the town its name was founded in 1080 by the eldest son of William the Conqueror, Robert Curthose, and built using earth and timber. Between 1168 and 1178 the castle as we know it today was rebuilt in stone. Today, iron sculptures of medieval archers guard the Castle Keep, as did English armies in the wars against Scotland.

On Boxing Day, 1292, John Balliol, King of Scots, visited and reportedly paid homage to King Edward I, the 'Hammer of the Scots' in the great hall of the fortress. Later, the castle was the last line of defence when the town was besieged during the English Civil War, eventually falling to Scottish forces allied with Parliament in October, 1644. Graffiti from the time of this stand-off can still be found inside the Keep. From the 16th century to around 1812, the cellar of the Keep was used as a prison for the county of Northumberland. Traces of the prisoners' chains are still attached to the walls.

Incredible to think, but in Victorian times the Keep was nearly demolished to make way for the expanding rail network. Thankfully, famed Newcastle architect John Dobson restored the building in 1848 and it was saved for future generations.

The Castle Keep and the Black Gate were reunited as a single attraction, Newcastle Castle, in 2015.

Slade were the biggest, loudest, most fun-packed pop band of their era and, on November 4, 1972, they were photographed rocking Newcastle City Hall to its foundations.

The boys from Wolverhampton, fronted by gravel-throated Noddy Holder, were the hottest group of the time and the finest purveyors of so-called 'glam rock'.

Any pop fan who lived through the first half of the 1970s will remember Slade fondly. The band's deliberately misspelled song titles had English teachers pulling their hair out, but the records sold like hot cakes. Cum On Feel The Noize, Skweeze Me Pleeze Me, Coz I Luv You, Look Wot You Dun, Take Me Back 'Ome and Mama Weer All Crazee Now were all huge hits in an era when Slade , and the likes of T Rex, Sweet and David Bowie, cheered up a nation struggling with endless strikes and inflation.

A Chronicle concert review of the band at Newcastle City Hall from a couple of years later, in May 1974, vividly captured Slade -mania. The reporter wrote: "Pop fans in Newcastle ran wild last night as Slade hit the city .

"Followers inside the City Hall stormed the stage, while other fans locked out of the sold-out concert smashed windows and stormed doors to get in. Hysterical girls were helped out of the hall , overcome with emotion. Some fans were even jumping down from the balconies on to the stage."

After the show, hundreds of fans gathered outside the City Hall and were joined by Newcastle United supporters fresh from a testimonial game at St James' Park to chant: "Howay the Slade" and "We want Slade". The band, of course, was managed by ex-Animal Chas Chandler, who'd also discovered Jimi Hendrix in 1966. Noddy Holder, famed for the mirrored top hat and raucous singing voice, told the Chronicle in 1975: "Chas was able to steer us past the pitfalls that had trapped The Animals. In many ways we have had it easier than they did back in the 1960s."

When Chas Chandler died in 1996, the former members of Slade attended his funeral. Noddy Holder quit the band in 1992, but various versions of the group have continued to perform.

It was July 20, 1972 and the Scotswood Aggro Boys were out and about. Only this time the feared gang from Newcastle's West End were doing their good deed for the day, having organised a disco to raise funds for children with disabilities.

The early 1970s saw youth gangs emerge across the towns of suburban Tyneside and the North East. They would fight rival gangs, marking out their territories out with graffiti tags. It was the era of the Doctor Marten-wearing, reggae-loving skinhead.

Over at Newcastle United's St James' Park where the often edgy atmosphere was utterly different to today's match day experience, the gangs would congregate in the long-demolished Leazes End causing all sorts of mayhem.

The Scotswood Aggro Boys had actually featured in a BBC documentary aired in 1971. Called 'All Dressed Up And Going Nowhere', it was filmed in Newcastle and records their conflicts with a rival gang of motorbike-driving 'hairies'. Amid graffiti-scarred streets, we see the skinheads on the prowl, young lads tearing down the back lanes of old Benwell on home-made 'bogies', and Dunston Power Station pumping out smoke across the Tyne. Meanwhile, the hairies are filmed tearing around Newcastle city centre on impressive motorbikes in an age before wearing safety helmets became compulsory.

The film, narrated by a certain Mike Neville, was out of circulation for years, but popped up on YouTube a while back. It's the portrait of an often vanished city, and it's well worth a watch. It talks of "violent crime escalating, despite the emergence of shiny office blocks and new estates in Newcastle with a new way of life breeding a new way of violence".

A few years ago, the BBC revisited 'All Dressed Up And Going Nowhere', and met some of the lads as they are today - grandparents in their early 60s.

A night out in Newcastle - a scene that's been replayed countless times over the generations. Three young women in their glad-rags pose for the camera on the city's Newgate Street, next to the now-demolished Newgate shopping centre. Clearly maxi-dresses, flares, and platform boots were all the rage then. The picture was taken by a roving Chronicle photographer on the night of Sunday, October 22, 1972. The young women will all be in their 60s today.

Wearing his parka – a favourite kids' fashion item of the time – this young reader chooses a book at Low Fell library, Gateshead, in January 1972. Wonder if he ever became an astronaut?

October 1972, and the sound of music was in the air… David Cassidy was number one in the charts with How Can I Be Sure. There were also big hits for Slade with Mama Weer All Crazee Now; The Sweet with Wig-Wam Bam; and Lieutenant Pigeon with the highly forgettable Mouldy Old Dough.

But it was also a time the streets and playing fields of North East housing estates would resound to the unmistakable sound of kazoos and drums. This was the golden age of home-grown juvenile marching jazz bands when songs like When The Saints Go Marching In and the theme tune to Z-Cars were high on the repertoire of any self-respecting band.

On Sunday, October 8, 1972, some of Tyneside's leading jazz bands competed to be crowned best in the region.

The Evening Chronicle reported: "The weather was brilliant and the entertainment was fantastic as the North's 10 best bands battled for the title of the region's top band at Brough Park Stadium in Newcastle.

"The bands had fought through a succession of preliminary competitions all summer to earn the right to compete for the title, and nearly 8,000 spectators turned up to see who would win.

"The winning band was the South Shields Golden Eagles who soared away with the title, although it took all of four hours of marching and music to claim the victory . . . and only by the tiniest of margins.

"Runners-up were the Felling Fusiliers (who are pictured) and they just pipped eight other superb bands. The competition and standard set was top class."

The bands, featuring nearly 1,000 children in brightly coloured uniforms, marched to the beat of 100 drums through the streets of Newcastle to reach the Byker greyhound racing venue, which is called Newcastle Stadium today.

As well as South Shields Golden Eagles and Felling Fusiliers, other bands included Walker Majestics, Simonside Mariners, Wallsend Rising Sun Legionnaires, Howdon Hussars, Willington Revellers, and the Old Tyme Has Beens Jazz Band.

How many of these bands survive today, we wonder?

A Tyne foyboatman at work, Mill Dam, South Shields, 1972. This would have been a common sight on the River Tyne for generations. A foyboat was a small vessel used to help larger ships and boats when they needed to be moored or serviced.

Birtley sits to the south of Gateshead. This was its new shopping centre in 1972.

Two hundred years earlier when John Wesley visited in 1743, he described Birtley as "surrounded by collieries on every side". This situation continued until the 1960s when the industry began to decline. The last coal mined in Gateshead was at Marley Hill Colliery near Whickham. The pit closed in 1983.

Other prominent industries in the area in the last century and a half included brick-making and an iron works, while salt was important way back in the 1600s and 1700s.

As for day-to-day life in Birtley, the Birtley Co-operative Society - or "the store" - began life in 1861, and had premises first in Mount Pleasant, then in Durham Road, then from 1885 at Harras Bank. There was a disastrous fire at this store on Christmas morning in 1900, and the shop eventually re-opened in new permanent premises on Durham Road.

As for recreation, there was once horse-racing in the area which included a steeplechase in Birtley in 1845.

When Germany launched its brutal invasion of Belgium at the start of World War I, many Belgians ended up here, living in Elisabethville, a small settlement away from the town. The men were employed at a munitions works, making shells for use mainly on the Western Front.

Staff work by candle light and hurricane lamps in the newsroom of the Newcastle Chronicle and Journal on February 12, 1972. Power cuts early in the decade were part of an era of industrial strife, which saw government and trade unions repeatedly going head to head. This round of power cuts was brought about by a national miners' strike. Work had stopped at all 289 pits in England and Wales on January 9.

As the strike wore on, and coal supplies at power stations ran low, factories and businesses closed as the Government was forced to impose a three-day working week. Many of the nation's homes and businesses would be without electricity for up to nine hours a day.

After seven crippling weeks, the miners returned to work on February 24 and the lights went back on - for the time being. There would be more power cuts to come.

Newcastle United's superstar centre-forward Malcolm Macdonald was at St James' Park modelling clothes from his newly-opened Newcastle boutique with his then business partner Alan Owen and Evening Chronicle reporter Claire on May 9, 1972. The shop, specialising in men's clothes, was called For The Exclusive Man and was situated in the city's Newgate Shopping Centre. Opened in 1969, the centre was torn down in 2016 to make way for a new £100m hotel, flats and shopping complex.

This attractive building with Portland stone columns on the corner of Newcastle's Pilgrim and Market Streets was photographed on an unseasonably mild day, December 21, 1972.

Opened in 1934, the site was home to the city's fire station, police station and magistrates' court until vacated in the mid-2000s.

The grade II-listed building was set in 2018 to feature in regeneration plans for Pilgrim Street as the area became a reborn leisure and retail sector.

Hundreds of fans besieged Newcastle City Hall on May 20, 1972, desperate to get their hands on tickets for T Rex's upcoming show on the Electric Warrior tour. These great images show teenage pop fans dressed in the groovy fashions of the era. Duffle coats, velvet jackets, platform boots, cheesecloth shirts, and velvet loons were the must-wear items for the youth of the day. And everybody had long hair - men and women.

T Rex – fronted by the charismatic Marc Bolan - would roll into Newcastle a month later on Saturday June 24, during a nationwide jaunt that would also take in Manchester Belle Vue ballroom and Birmingham Odeon as well as the cavernous Wembley Empire Pool (later Wembley Arena) which had just started hosting giant rock shows.

T Rex would play two short performances at the City Hall - one at 6pm, the other at 8.30pm. Tickets were just 75p - around £9.75 in today's money.

At both shows, pandemonium reportedly ensued as the scarf-waving, mainly female audiences screamed throughout, while at the later show, there were repeated attempts by fans to storm the stage and get closer to their idol.

In 1972, T Rex were at the peak of their powers. They enjoyed their final number one, Metal Guru, in May and their last top ten hit, The Groover, came in June the following year. In September 1977, Bolan was killed in a car crash, two weeks before his 30th birthday.

The unmistakeable 'brutalist' concrete structure of Gateshead's Trinity Square multi-storey car park on May 25, 1972. Designed by London architect Owen Luder, it was nicknamed the 'Get Carter Car Park' after its appearance in the 1971 film. Everything in this photograph is now demolished.

The unmistakable curve of the River Tyne - with the high-rise cityscape of Newcastle in the distance.

Today things are quieter, but back on January 6, 1972, when our image was captured, the Tyne was still a busy working river. Taken from the Gateshead side, we see a ship berthed just over the water at Spillers, with the cranes hard at work.

Completed in 1938, the giant flour mill supplied the baking industry for decades, including making flour for Greggs. The site was also where Home Pride flour was made, famous for Fred, their bowler-hatted mascot. Remember the 1970s television adverts? Wheat arrived here from Europe, Canada, the US and Australia.

At its peak in the 1970s more than 500 staff worked here providing the flour for one in every 10 loaves baked in the UK. Operations ceased in 2007, but unlike another former flour mill building upriver - the Baltic - which was re-purposed as a modern art gallery, the iconic Spillers structure was bulldozed in 2011.

The site would later host the annual Evolution music festival while, in 2015, the Newcastle Chronicle reported how planning chiefs had given the nod to the building of a £10m sub-sea engineering test centre.

A chilly-looking scene at North Shields railway station on April 6, 1972. There had been a station here since 1839. In 1890 it was expanded to include new booking offices, which in turn were replaced by this fabricated structure in the mid-1960s. The station closed in August 1980, reopening – like many other former railway stations – as a stop on the new Tyneside Metro system in November, 1982.

Two young boys play amid the looming high-rise tower blocks at Cruddas Park Housing Estate in Newcastle, May 23, 1972.

Another traditional Newcastle watering hole, the Trafalgar Hotel, bit the dust in 1972. Newcastle Chronicle photographers captured the old pub, on the corner of Trafalgar Street and New Bridge Street, being demolished on April 4 of that year. The pub had been a favourite since 1879 and was described as "one of Newcastle beer drinkers' most cherished haunts".

The newspaper reporter, however, chided the health and safety - or lack it - at the location. Without warning, the building dramatically collapsed on to the street, and workmen narrowly avoided injury from flying debris.

Today you'll find a Premier Inn hotel on the site.

1973

Had you been out and about in the Tyne Valley on October 23, 1973, you might have seen two familiar faces and a BBC film crew among the winding country lanes.

Actors James Bolam and Rodney Bewes were happily shooting on location in the heart of rural Northumberland for the second series of Whatever Happened To The Likely Lads?

The ever-popular series featuring the exploits of two thirtysomething pals – Terry Collier and Bob Ferris - was set on Tyneside and was penned by the brilliant writing team of Whitley Bay-born Ian le Frenais and sidekick Dick Clement.

The Likely Lads first emerged in the 1960s, and we meet them again in the 1970s, older but not always wiser.

While series one of 'Whatever' re-united Terry and Bob after the former's stint in the Army, series two saw Bob newly-married to the formidable Thelma and struggling to reconcile new-found domesticity to his long-term friendship with Jack-the-lad, Terry.

While Bob aspired to the new upwardly-mobile pretensions of the decade – badminton clubs, dinner parties and cut-and-blow hairstyles - Terry harked back to a world of beer, birds and lads' nights out.

The series reflected rapidly changing times in a changing region.

In the autumn of 1973 they were filming location scenes for the episode "Affairs and Relations", a typical British farce in which the pair go fishing, only to find Thelma's dad 'playing away' with his blonde secretary in the same hotel. Meanwhile, an amorous barmaid makes a play for Terry, just as Thelma turns up unexpectedly to spark a series of accusations and misunderstandings. Classic 1970s comedy.

The episode is set in the Barrasford Arms Hotel, in the Northumberland village of the same name. It's a lovely pub, and well worth a visit, as is the Dipton Mill Inn which is also featured and where we see hen-pecked Bob in the phone box making yet another call home to Thelma. We also see the lads fishing in the North Tyne near the Northumberland village of Humshaugh.

Sadly, the series would be last we'd see of the Likely Lads – other than a 1976 feature film – and a reported fall-out between Bewes and Bolam at the time put paid to any future reunion. The pair never spoke again.

In recent years, Rodney Bewes said of the fall-out: "Yes, it's very sad – especially as the show is remembered with so much affection."

And was there ever any chance of a reunion?

"No, never. The problem is that Jimmy (Bolam) hates the show. He feels it diminishes him as an actor. And I don't understand it because it's such a fantastic part, penned by brilliant writers. It's so sad."

Rodney Bewes died on November 21, 2017, six days before his 80th birthday at his seaside home in Cornwall.

Barrow boys selling fruit and vegetables in Newcastle city centre on August 3, 1973. At the time, 1lb of apple would have knocked you back about 14p.

The elegant Gibside Chapel in 1973. The chapel is today part of a large, scenic National Trust estate that sits on the outskirts of the former industrial Tyneside. It is located between Rowlands Gill and Burnopfield. Tracing its origins back to the early 16th century, the estate was later owned by the Bowes-Lyons and visited on several occasions by the Queen Mother who was a family member.

Still one of Newcastle's most pleasing classical-style buildings, this was the headquarters of the Northumberland and Durham Trustee Savings Bank on the corner of Grainger Street and Westgate Road on January 11, 1973. Today, like many former banks and finance houses in the city centre, the Victorian-era building plays host to a popular bar.

Newcastle United midfielder Jimmy Smith in action against Liverpool at St James' Park on April 21, 1973. Nicknamed Jinky, the Glaswegian-born crowd favourite's game was characterised by superb ball skills, mazy dribbles, cheeky 'nutmegs', the ability to turn a match, and a deceptively languid style. Signed for a reported £100,000 amid a welter of press publicity in the summer of 1969, Jinky's career was cut short by a knee injury and he was forced to hang up his boots in 1976, aged just 29. As for this 1973 game against Liverpool, United won 2-1, with John Tudor scoring twice in front of a crowd of 36,810.

Mike Neville was the friendly face of TV news in the North East for four decades. A brilliant presenter, he had the unique ability to convey every story in an appropriate manner, be it serious or light-hearted. There was genuine sadness across the region when news of his death at the age of 80 was reported in September, 2017.

Mike (real name Jimmy Briggs) was born in Willington Quay, North Tyneside, in October, 1936. Before he left school at 15, he had his first shot at acting, fulfilling an ambition he'd held since childhood.

He then applied to be a junior for the Daily Mail in Newcastle and did well in the job for 18 months before being called up for his two years' National Service. Getting his break in television, Mike became one of the most famous faces in the North East, working firstly with ITV, then the BBC, and for the last decade of his career, back with ITV.

After starting out at Tyne Tees TV, Mike Neville was Mr BBC for 32 years, presenting Look North and a range of network programmes, including the popular Nationwide.

He would turn down many offers of work in London. His on-screen banter with fellow Beeb presenter George House (the pair are pictured together in December, 1973) livened up many an episode of Look North – and as a man of many talents, Mike once even presented Come Dancing.

Over the years he rubbed shoulders with many greats from the worlds of TV and sport.

In 1990 he was awarded an MBE for services to television. It was just one of many gongs Mike picked up during his career. One of his many fans was former Prime Minister, Tony Blair, who described the presenter as "one of the great unifiers" of the North East.

In June 2006, Mike Neville announced his retirement. This coincided with Tyne Tees' cost-cutting move from City Road to a single news studio in Gateshead. Mike's personality was far bigger than the new studio, with him famously quipping: "Welcome to the broom cupboard!"

It truly was the end of an era when he signed off for the final time.

At the time of his retirement, the Newcastle Chronicle declared: "Mike Neville is a legend – the face of North East television news for more than 40 years.

"He has no equals. Generations have grown up with Mike whether it be BBC Look North or Tyne Tees. We wish him well."

Rock superstar David Bowie was performing at Newcastle City Hall near the end of his marathon Ziggy Stardust tour on June 2, 1973. The iconic performer had appeared at the same venue a year earlier and would return for a trio of celebrated gigs at the same venue in June 1978. Later he would grace Sunderland's Roker Park in 1987, Newcastle Mayfair in 1991, Newcastle Riverside in 1997, and he was the first major artist to appear at Newcastle Arena in 1995.

One of the giant cultural figures of his age, music fans around the world were stunned in January 2016, when it was announced Bowie had passed away. The 69-year-old singer's illness had been kept secret and news that he'd died shocked his legions of followers.

Calling at Newcastle Central Station on July 19, 1973 was Locomotive 41001. British Rail's high speed train – along with its twin Locomotive 41002 – was capable of travelling from Newcastle to London in three hours at speeds of over 140mph.

Newcastle office workers enjoy a sunny lunch break in a pleasant city centre churchyard during the summer of 1973. St John the Baptist, on the corner of Westgate Road and Grainger Street, was one of the old town's four original parish churches, along with All Saints, St Nicholas', and St Andrew's. Dating back to around 1287, St John's – which would once have stood in open countryside – has been ever-present as Newcastle grew and prospered over the centuries into the modern, post-industrial city it is today.

A long-time retail favourite destination, this was the C&A clothing store in Princess Square, Newcastle, on November 22, 1973. The company had begun trading in 1922. Going the same way as the likes of Woolworth and BHS, in June 2000 C&A announced it was to close all its UK stores with the loss of 4,800 jobs.

Jarrow's Arndale Arcade in 1973.
The pedestrianised shopping centre, opened in 1961, was one of the first of its kind in the UK. It is still popular with shoppers today.

(Picture used courtesy of Paul Perry)

At a time when the Tyne was still busy, the cruise ship Vistafjord was leaving the river after her sea trials in April 1973. Built at Swan Hunter's Neptune yard in Low Walker, the vessel served as a popular passenger ship for many years. After being renamed a number of times, then nearly becoming a floating hotel in 2014, the Vistafjord was broken up at Alang in India in 2017.

Staff and pupils at an unnamed school in Felling, Gateshead on March 22, 1973, wearing the fashions of the era.

It was a time-honoured Tyneside scene as crowds flocked to Newcastle Quayside's Sunday market on August 5, 1973. The market was first mentioned in records from 1736, but is thought to date from centuries earlier.

Newcastle is famous for its historic markets, some of which survive to this day.

If the Grainger Market and Bigg Market are still with us, the Groat Market, Flesh Market, Cloth Market, White Cross Market, Herb Market, Fish Market and Greenmarket have all vanished.

In 1770, Newcastle was said to be "provided with all kinds of provision from the very plentiful markets of the town, here being used annually above 5,000 beeves, 10,000 calves, 143,000 sheep and lambs, with swine, fish, poultry, eggs, butter in a prodigious abundance".

As for the Quayside Sunday market, it's had its ups and downs over the years. As the Newcastle Chronicle reported in 2007, it needed a major relaunch after struggling for trade. Thankfully, the Quayside is now busy with stalls and shoppers every Sunday.

Back in the early 18th century it stretched from the old Tyne Bridge (where the Swing Bridge is today) to Sandgate (near where the Millennium Bridge is today). It would have been a vibrant mix of market stalls, racing tipsters and fairground attractions. In Victorian times, fortune tellers, escapologists, and strongman acts would have pulled in the crowds.

Meanwhile, in 2004, one Chronicle reader recalled her Shieldfield childhood memories of 1930s Sunday Quayside markets. She said: "The stall-keepers were all characters with the gift of the gab. We always lingered at the stall that sold sweets. Every so often they'd have a throw-out of sweets into the crowd and there'd be a mad scramble.

"Another stall sold crockery. This man never stopped talking about his wares. When he came to the plates and saucers he'd juggle them in the air, talking all the time.

"Another stall sold medicine and pills, and there was some sort of rubbing oil.

"A man would strip to his waist. He would rub the oil over his body and arms until his skin was shimmering.

"Then he started rippling his muscles, especially his arms and, at the same time he'd be telling everyone the oil he was using would get rid of all his aches and pains and sprains.

"Boy, I could certainly do with some of that oil now," the 78-year-old joked at the time.

The Who were one of the biggest rock bands of the 1970s. In November 1973, they played three shows at the Odeon Cinema in Newcastle.

The band's members Roger Daltrey, John Entwistle, Pete Townshend and Keith Moon took time out to meet fans Sarah Smith and Linda Scott.

The band who recorded a host of classics including My Generation, Pinball Wizard, and Won't Get Fooled Again were almost as famous for smashing up their equipment and their off-stage antics as their music.

After one of the November 1973 shows, the Newcastle Chronicle reported: "The Who lived up to its reputation for violence on stage with an expensive display of guitar and amplifier smashing last night.

"The concert was stopped in chaos when Pete Townshend bawled out sound engineers, destroyed pre-recorded backing tapes, and smashed up equipment. It was a ridiculous display of violence."

The band, upset by ongoing sound problems, partied heavily later that night at the Five Bridges Hotel in Gateshead. The newspaper reported how "police went to the band's luxury suite in the early hours of the morning to investigate a reported disturbance."

Moon died in 1978, and Entwistle in 2002. In 2014, an older and wiser Daltrey and Townshend appeared at Newcastle Arena on The Who's 50th anniversary tour.

The last Riverside line train waiting for passengers at Willington Quay station on July 20, 1973. The Riverside Branch - as it was known by British Rail and by rail enthusiasts – deviated from the suburban line which ran from Newcastle to the Coast via Wallsend. It left the 'main line' just after it crossed the Ouseburn Viaduct at Byker and followed the course of the Tyne, mainly serving shipyard workers. It rejoined the 'main line' at Percy Main.

The stations on the Riverside Branch were Byker, St Peters, St Anthonys, Walker, Carville, Point Pleasant and Willington Quay.

It closed in July 1973, but most of the route continued to be used sporadically by goods trains until 1978, with the final Western end continuing for scrap metal trains from St Peters right up to 1987. Most of the route is now a cycle track, particularly near Wallsend.

A young mother with her three young children at the notorious Noble Street flats complex in Newcastle's West End on a chilly December 7, 1973.

Past meets present in Grange Road, Jarrow in 1973. On the right, the relatively new high-rise and low-rise housing that characterised the era. Further up the road, on the right is the Town Hall, from where the men of the famous Jarrow Crusade set off on their march to London in 1936.

In the distance, the towering Christ Church, built in 1868, and a Grade II-listed structure.

And, on the left, the Regal Cinema. It had opened – in a former Salvation Army hall - as The Kino in 1908 as the new phenomenon of cinema began to spread like wildfire. A popular venue for many decades, the Regal closed in the 1970s and the building was demolished.

(Picture used courtesy of Paul Perry)

1974

Children from St Joseph's Primary School, Gateshead, were tucking into Quality Street chocolates at the nearby Five Bridges Hotel in May, 1974. These youngsters would have enjoyed more pocket money than their parents' generation did. If Quality Street are still popular today, a whole range of 1970s confectionery has been consigned to history. Who remembers Spangles, Aztecs, Amazin' Raisin Bars, Old Jamaica, and Fry's Five Centres from a long list of 'lost' '70s sweets and chocolate - not to mention Tyneside-produced Tudor Crisps?

This was Newcastle's Bigg Market in 1974. The object in the centre of the picture is the Rutherford Memorial Fountain. It stands in honour of John Hunter Rutherford, a Victorian-era doctor, educational reformer, and temperance campaigner. The monument has been around the block a couple of times. In 1903 to accommodate the new statue of recently deceased Queen Victoria, it was moved from its original spot outside St Nicholas' Cathedral to the Bigg Market. It was later moved from just beside the former gents' public toilets to its current spot further up the Bigg Market.

Workers in 1974 were rushing to buy that night's Evening Chronicle on their way out of the Parsons factory on Shields Road, Heaton, Newcastle. The iconic firm, founded by Charles Parsons in 1889, built dozens of turbines every year on this site. From the 1960s onwards, the company was involved in a series of mergers with the likes of Reyrolle and Clarke Chapman as the make-up of the industry changed. Today, work continues at this location in the shape of the giant Siemens organisation, which operates in the key sectors of energy, industry and healthcare.

A bleak December day in 1974, as we see litter and rubbish lying around Jarrow Shopping Centre in the midst of a council workers' strike.

South Shields railway station on February 3, 1974. Opened in 1879, it was operational for more than a century until 1981 and the dawn of the new Tyne and Wear Metro system. Steam trains at first, then electric trains from 1938, then diesel trains from 1963, travelled up and down between the seaside town and Newcastle. The Metro began running to South Shields in March, 1984, to a new station just yards to the west of the old one. The old station building was demolished in the late 1990s.

Another day in 1974 and more industrial action. A National Miners Strike took place that year, after a pay offer was rejected. It would foreshadow the momentous year-long national strike of a decade later. Pickets outside the National Coal Board headquarters at Team Valley, Gateshead, were persuading workers not to cross the picket line on February 11. This was the time of the 'three-day week' when Ted Heath's Tory government battled to conserve dwindling coal stock and thus electricity. The crisis lasted from January until early March and saw television going off air early, and pubs close their doors.

This was Newcastle's Geordie Pride pub in August 1974. It sat underneath a new office block and was part of a major 1971 redevelopment project. The well-known Douglas Hotel which had stood on the corner of Grainger Street and Neville Street, opposite Newcastle Central Station, had been demolished to make way. The new 8,000 square-feet underground drinking hole was advertised as 'the region's only walkabout pub'. It featured a reproduction of a Victorian Street, while the Douglas Hotel buffet of 100 years earlier was replicated, as seen in our photograph, 12 feet below where it once stood. The Geordie Pride closed in 1981.

(Opposite) Three images from Newcastle United's momentous - but ultimately doomed - 1974 FA Cup campaign.

We see the wives and girlfriends of the players before the big day, and the aftermath of the game when United returned home without the trophy. They may have been empty-handed but were still welcomed by huge crowds on the streets of Newcastle when they toured on an open-topped bus on a route that culminated at St James' Park.

The 1974 FA Cup final between Newcastle United took place at Wembley Stadium on Saturday, May 4. It was a game in which, after battling bravely and sometimes brilliantly on the road to Wembley, the Magpies simply failed to show up. The Scousers, spearheaded by a certain Kevin Keegan, ran out comfortable 3-0 winners.

It was a pivotal encounter.

On the day, United and Liverpool were more or less neck-and-neck in terms of major trophies won. For the Reds, the victory would herald a long, golden age of domestic and European domination. For the Magpies, the defeat was a major shock to the system.

The club hadn't lost an FA Cup final since 1911 - and had never lost one at Wembley. The defeat would signal the exit of Joe Harvey a year later, and the break-up of his team.

It would also begin a period of decline at Newcastle United which wouldn't be arrested until the Hall-Keegan era of 20 years later.

For its vast army of passionate supporters, the club would also now become perennial 'sleeping giants', 'nearly men' and 'also-rans' - descriptions which apply to this day.

The run-up to the final of 1974 had been so different. Malcolm Macdonald - all sideburns and swagger - was the undisputed king of Tyneside.

Backed by a talented supporting cast including Terry Hibbitt, Jimmy Smith and Bobby Moncur, the Cup run gathered momentum like a juggernaut as each round progressed.

This was a time before the all-consuming Premier League would dominate the domestic game. The FA Cup was still much-treasured, and Tyneside approached fever pitch as United disposed of their opponents one by one. Non-league Hendon, then Scunthorpe were sent packing after replays.

A superb 3-0 win at West Bromwich Albion was followed by one of the most dramatic games ever seen at St James' Park.

In front of 52,000 fans United, 3-1 down and reduced to 10 men, battled back to win 4-3 and send the Gallowgate crowd into meltdown.

The small matter of a pitch invasion by fans forced the FA to declare the result null and void, but two replays at Everton's Goodison Park finally saw United in the semi-final.

This would be Supermac's finest hour - his two fine goals at Hillsborough taking United past Burnley.

This was it. We believed. Six-time FA Cup winners United were heading back to Wembley. It had been Sunderland's turn in 1973. This year would be ours.

Then came the dismal defeat.

(Ironically, only months later the same two teams would meet again in the league at St James' Park. On this occasion, Macdonald and co ran riot, thrashing Liverpool 4-1).

Two days after the final, beaten United returned home to a heroes' welcome as tens of thousands of fans lined the streets of Newcastle and filled St James' Park.

Imagine what would happen if they ever won anything? The wait goes on.

Pensioners were queueing outside Greggs Seconds Shop, on Newcastle's Westgate Road in July 1974. The bakery goods were imperfectly baked and often mis-shaped but perfectly edible. Pensioners were allowed to buy bread at half price.

Greggs has evolved as a Tyneside institution over the last 80 years or so. Formerly known as Greggs of Gosforth, the company was founded by John Gregg and baked its first stottie cakes on the eve of World War II in 1939.

The first shop opened in 1951 in Gosforth and since then the company has gone from strength to strength. Starting from its Geordie base, Greggs has expanded nationally since the 1970s by adding other regional bakery chains to its roster.

After acquiring bread-making firms from Glasgow to Manchester, and Yorkshire to Kent, Greggs became top of the baps when it bought up its main rival Bakers Oven in 2008. For a short time, you could even buy a pease pudding stottie in Belgium where Greggs had ten stores for a time.

In 2018, there were more than 1,600 Greggs stores nationwide.

A young mother prepares to cross Westgate Road to get to Newcastle General Hospital in October 1974. Countless patients were cared for here over the decades.

The hospital was opened in 1870 to treat the sick of Newcastle's Workhouse complex. It was known as the Workhouse Infirmary or Union Hospital. It became Newcastle General Hospital in 1930, and a nurses' home was opened opposite with a tunnel connecting it to the hospital.

During both world wars, military authorities took over the majority of beds with more than 22,000 patients treated during World War II.

In 1948 the General was transferred to the NHS and many smaller hospitals amalgamated with it - until the opening of the new Freeman Hospital in 1978 when many wards were transferred there.

In 2010 the General's Accident and Emergency department and Intensive Care unit closed - marking the end of an era.

A walk-in centre for minor ailments and injuries remains on the site, as does the Campus for Ageing and Vitality, and a Diabetes Centre.

A staple of North East life, a night at the local social club - in this picture we see the audience enjoying themselves at Westerhope Excelsior Social Club, Newcastle, in March 1974.

The rise of working men's clubs began in Victorian times, and at first they were intended to be educational and teetotal. However, working men - then as now - enjoyed a pint, and booze soon became available.

The North has traditionally been fond of its clubs, with Newcastle and Tyneside still boasting popular establishments serving good quality, lower-priced alcohol and entertainment.

Under the umbrella organisation of the CIU (The Working Men's Club and Institute Union) there are around 2,000 affiliated clubs across the country.

Until 2004, the CIU had its own beer brewed by the Federation brewery in Dunston, Gateshead.

Between 1974 and 1977, the ITV variety show The Wheeltappers and Shunters Social Club reflected the popularity of the local club. Featuring the likes of Bernard Manning and "concert chairman" Colin Crompton, the fictional club was actually based in a Manchester television studio.

Over the years, many talented musicians have learned their trades on the demanding stages of North East's clubland.

In recent times, however, working men's clubs have suffered from an old-fashioned image among younger people. Declining footfall has seen many clubs close.

Anti-smoking legislation has also no doubt had an impact, and it was only in recent years that women were allowed full CIU membership.

The Byker Wall has been a prominent, unmistakable part of Newcastle's cityscape since its construction in the 1970s. Here, we see part of the distinctive housing complex in 1974.

The estate began as a slum clearance project in 1969 and was completed in 1982.

The Wall, along with the low-rise homes built to its south, replaced Victorian-built terraced housing.

There were nearly 1,200 dilapidated houses in old Byker. They had been condemned as unfit for human habitation in 1953, but demolition did not begin until 1966.

Unlike most other housing estates thrown up in the 1960s and 1970s, the estate was actually Grade II listed in 2007. The eye-catching 1.3 mile-long development was designed by Swedish architect Ralph Erskine.

The focal point of the estate is the Byker Wall – a complex of 620 maisonettes – but the estate itself contains 2,000 properties, designed as five interlinking communities. The Wall and estate show strong Scandinavian influences, with the use of timber and bright colours, prompting some local folk to nickname it 'Legoland'.

Speaking about his work, Erskine once said: "The job of buildings is to improve human relations – architecture must ease them, not make them worse."

It was not just miners and council workers who were fighting for better pay and conditions in 1974. In May that year, under-paid nurses and health workers marched down Newcastle's Grainger Street protesting their grievances. 'Cinderella will go to the ball' and 'Give us what we deserve, a living wage' were just two of the memorable messages among the banners and placards.

Even schoolchildren went on strike in the 1970s…

Angry pupils stormed out of a Newcastle school one afternoon in November, 1974, in protest against having to wear school uniforms.

Several hundred fourth and fifth-formers at Kenton School ran from the school grounds, chanting as they went. A number of children fell to the ground when the pupils dashed down Drayton Road. Traffic came to a standstill as they blocked the road.

The pupils' leader said: "We have decided to strike – and we don't intend to come back until we get what we want."

He said that 15 and 16-year-olds did not like wearing uniforms but they were forced to. He also claimed the girls were not allowed to wear trousers in the winter. The antics attracted the attention of the Chronicle - and even local TV news cameras - before the pupils were persuaded to return to class.

Millions of waxed cartons went up in flames in a spectacular blaze in Newcastle, in October 1974. The fire ripped through the Co-operative Wholesale Society warehouse in Ford Street, Byker. Around 45 firemen tackled the blaze with the help of breathing apparatus, two hydraulic platforms and a turntable ladder. The one man who was working in the building, the warehouse foreman, sounded the alarm when the fire broke out at 3.30pm. He escaped unhurt but shocked. The waxed cartons belonged to the Bowaters company of the Team Valley Estate. They were mainly for milk supplies.

A stunning sight... Local people turned out to see off World Unicorn, a 257,000-tonne supertanker, as it left the River Tyne in early 1974. Built at Swan Hunter's Wallsend yard, it was launched in May 1973, by Princess Anne, and completed in February the following year. The ship's construction and launch would be the subject of a series of iconic photographs and a short colour film. The giant vessel was broken up in Kaohsiung, Taiwan in October 1984.

1975

(Top) A classic image from the Newcastle Chronicle archive.

Captured by staff photographer Tom Buist, it brilliantly sums up life in industrial Tyneside in the 1970s.

In the foreground a lad plays on the iconic bicycle of the day – a Raleigh Chopper. Behind him, the gigantic Tyne Pride is under construction. It overshadows the terraced Leslie Street in Wallsend, populated by shipbuilders and factory workers. The oil tanker was built at the Swan Hunter yard.

(Bottom) Launched in October 1975, as seen in our second image, and completed in November the following year, the ship was operational for the next four decades.

Later renamed several times, it was broken up at Chittagong in Bangladesh in 2005.

The popular Segedunum Roman Fort museum today stands on the site of demolished Leslie Street.

Tyne Dock in South Shields was busy with activity on this day in 1975.

When it opened in 1859, the River Tyne port area covered a sizeable 50 acres. At its height in 1913, seven million tons of coal were exported from here each year.

By 1923 there were around 170,000 miners working in the pits of the County Durham coalfield. Much of that coal made its way to Tyne Dock from where it was shipped to London or exported.

Coal arrived here on freight trains from the many mines dotted across County Durham. The railway lines crossed the Jarrow to South Shields road over five long-gone arches towards their destination of Tyne Dock. The coal was poured into collier ships from four staiths, using 42 spouts.

Today, Tyne Dock operates as part of the wider Port of Tyne, one of the UK's most innovative and efficient deep-sea ports handling cargoes across five continents.

Recognise any faces from the past? Hundreds of fans were waiting to see TV actor John Alderton and his actress wife Pauline Collins open a Newcastle fashion store in 1975. Alderton appeared in hit series such as Please Sir, My Wife Next Door and as the chauffeur in the early 20th century-set drama Upstairs, Downstairs opposite his wife.

Antiquity and modernity side by side in January, 1975. St John the Baptist church, which dates from the 13th century, has stood through the ages and remains an oasis of calm in the heart of busy Newcastle city centre. It is situated on the corner of Grainger Street and Westgate Road.

The looming multi-storey Westgate House office block built in 1972, meanwhile, was an unpopular architectural monstrosity. It represented much that was bad about planning and building in Newcastle in the 1960s and 70s.

Apart from being ugly in itself, it was completely unsympathetic to its surroundings, dwarfing and overshadowing the fine nearby Victorian constructions of the Central Station, Royal Station Hotel, the Lit and Phil Society and the Union Rooms.

St John's remains unchanged today. Westgate House was demolished in 2007.

A view of Newcastle's Cloth Market with its bars and restaurants in April 1975. One of those bars, of course, was Balmbra's which was immortalised in Geordie Ridley's Tyneside anthem, the Blaydon Races, written in 1862.

The Cloth Market was originally one of several medieval Newcastle markets clustered around St Nicholas' church (later cathedral). At the old Cloth Market, popular fairs were held every August and October when linen and blankets were sold ahead of the impending winter.

The area was also home to the Bigg Market, Flesh Market and Fish Market at different times, and traders found the nearby Lort Burn - which ran down where Grey Street and Dean Street are today - handy for throwing animal waste into. It smelled badly, apparently!

Four young lads show off their prize goldfish at the Hoppings in the summer of 1975.

The travelling funfair takes place on Newcastle's Town Moor every year. It started life in 1882 as a temperance fair at a time when Victorian do-gooders across the country chose to preach the virtues of being tee-total. The event was designed to be a counter-attraction to the boozy goings-on at the annual Race Week at nearby Newcastle Racecourse.

It was an instant hit. A newspaper report from the time read: "On whatever part of the moor the eye rested, a moving mass of human beings was witnessed."

The name Hoppings is thought to derive from the hopping, or dancing, that often took place at old fairs, (but it was not until the 1950s that the Hoppings became the universally recognised title of the yearly Tyneside event).

The First World War saw the fair move to Jesmond Dene between 1914 and 1918. The end of hostilities saw its return to the Town Moor. There were no Hoppings in the early 1920s but they returned in 1924, continuing through the years with a bumper record attendance in 1947.

Today it is a much-loved Tyneside institution, annually attracting around 300,000 visitors during its week-long stay.

If you were a teenage girl in the mid-70s, you were more than likely a fan of the Bay City Rollers.

Ten years after Beatlemania, the five-piece Edinburgh pop band sparked similar scenes of mass hysteria across Britain.

Lacking the long-term impact of the Fab Four, Rollermania came and went quickly but sparked a whole lot of screaming among hordes of tartan-clad teenybopper fans.

The Rollers arrived at Newcastle City Hall on May 7, 1975, with Bye Bye Baby, their biggest ever hit, sitting at the top of the singles charts. Pandemonium followed with a reviewer for the Chronicle declaring: "Only the group could hear the music they played - it was impossible to find out the number they were performing.

"Soon, the front stage area was a swaying mass of girls, six-deep, each struggling to get on to the stage.

"It became more like a riot. I saw girls trampled in the crush, before a row of seats buckled under the orderless crowd.

"The Rollers played their last number - and ran."

The Osmonds were one of the biggest pop bands of the early 1970s, attracting hordes of teenage female fans.

The clean-cut American family hailed from Utah.

From 1971 to 1975, both as The Osmonds and with Donny singing solo, they had hits including Crazy Horses, Love Me For a Reason, Puppy Love, and The Twelfth Of Never. Sister Marie Osmond had a solo hit with Paper Roses, as did younger brother Jimmy with Long Haired Lover From Liverpool.

It was at Newcastle City Hall as late as 1980 that The Osmonds in their entirety first played in the region. The group had previously concentrated their UK gigs in London and the North West.

Back in May, 1975, these Gateshead schoolgirls were set to celebrate their 15th birthdays alongside 18,000 other fans as they headed to London's cavernous Earls Court to see the Osmonds in concert.

In 2018, various Osmonds acts were still performing - Donny and Marie as a duo, while Jimmy, Jay and Merrill were going out as a trio. Alan's sons were also performing as a second-generation Osmonds.

An aerial view of Newcastle's Swan House roundabout in 1975. Swan House was built between 1963 and 1969, and traffic on the busy Central Motorway runs underneath it. Named after famous North East scientist and inventor of the light bulb, Joseph Swan, the office block became home to the GPO and then BT. Constructed on the site of John Dobson's Royal Arcade shopping complex, built in 1831-32, Swan House was voted one of Tyneside's biggest eyesores in 1998. Amid the roar of traffic, the multi-storey tower block is now called 55 degrees North and is home to executive apartments and a restaurant.

A very different St James' Park to the 52,000-capacity, state-of-the-art, all-seater stadium that is home to Newcastle United today.

Back in 1975, supporters stood in the roofless Gallowgate End, or the opposite Leazes End which had acquired a roof back in 1929. The East Stand was a recent addition, being constructed in 1972.

The old West Stand, home to the players' changing rooms and boardroom, dated back to 1906 and was built in the midst of United's golden Edwardian era. The four giant floodlight pylons erected in 1958 were city-centre landmarks for the next two decades.

The old ground was certainly looking a bit ramshackle by 1975, but could generate an electric atmosphere on its day.

Crowds flocked to Tyneside Summer Exhibition, Newcastle in 1975. Held on the Town Moor, the annual event ran from the early 1960s to 1987. On the same site, it followed in the footsteps of the Royal Jubilee Exhibition of 1887 commemorating Queen Victoria's 50 years on the throne. Two million people visited. Later, in 1929, another massive event - the North East Coast Exhibition - took place there. Opened by the Prince of Wales – later King Edward VIII – it ran from May to October and aimed to boost the region's trade and employment at a time of economic woe.

This was the Queen Elizabeth hospital, high up in Sheriff Hill, Gateshead, in 1975.

Today, one of the North East's leading centres for healthcare, it has cared for generations of patients.

But it all began more modestly. The QE started life as a small, infectious diseases isolation hospital in the late 19th century.

A plan to radically extend the hospital was mooted in 1938, but building work was interrupted by World War II. The bulk of the work continued slowly, not being completed until 1945.

The hospital is named after Queen Elizabeth (later the Queen Mother) who officially opened the extensions on Thursday, March 18, 1948. She met nurses and doctors - and visited the maternity unit.

In 1944 there had been 645 births in the hospital. In 1947 that rose to 844. And in 1947 it increased again to 870. The main hospital saw 2,225 patients admitted to the general ward during 1947.

A report into the hospital soon after its opening declared: "The co-operation and team spirit of the staff is not the least remarkable feature of a hospital that has given just cause for satisfaction and pride to the citizens of Gateshead."

Moving forward, there were improvements at the QE in 1967 with the addition of an outpatients department, an A&E department, a new operating theatre, and a medical records department.

But, showing how times and attitudes have changed, in the same year there were separate dining rooms for nurses and consultants who weren't allowed to mix during their lunch breaks!

Today, the QE provides cutting-edge treatment, including a £32m emergency care centre, a £12m pathology centre of excellence, and the Peter Smith Surgery Centre, which aims to give patients the same care experience - including en-suite facilities - you would expect from a 5-star hotel.

New Zealand athlete, Rod Dixon, chases down local favourite Brendan Foster in the 5,000 metres at the Rediffusion Gateshead Games at Gateshead Youth Stadium, on July 26, 1975. Today it's better known as Gateshead International Stadium. The venue would gain national and international fame as the home of the Gateshead Games - annual top-class athletics meetings which ran for some years and attracted track and field stars from around the globe. It was Foster - a former schoolteacher and an Olympic bronze medallist in 1976 - who was the inspiration for these, and the later Great North Run.

Over the middle decades of the last century, Gateshead boasted a host of cinemas - the Ritz, the Essoldo, the Palace, the Classic, the Empress, the Palladium, the Scala, the Shipcote, and others.

All of these once-thriving picture halls have come and gone, taking a host of memories with them.

But it was the Odeon that shone brightest in Gateshead during the heyday of the cinema. Back on February 15, 1937, Gracie Fields - one of the nation's biggest singing, comedy and acting stars - officially opened the opulent new picture house.

Originally known as Black's Regal, the cinema was taken over by the Odeon chain in 1944, before being re-named Gateshead Odeon a year later.

Fields, at the time, was Britain's highest-paid music and film star, and interrupted a holiday in glamorous St Moritz to come to chilly Tyneside for the occasion. Thousands lined the High Street, and traffic was halted as 'the Rochdale Lass' sang on the cinema roof.

The Odeon was Gateshead's finest cinema and boasted an impressive Compton organ which was played during performances and intervals. For decades the grand, old cinema attracted generations of movie-goers before its gradual decline and closure.

Our photo was taken in 1975, years after the cinema's glory days. We can see the 1974 action film Thunderbolt and Lightfoot, starring Clint Eastwood and Jeff Bridges, was showing at the time. This was an era when the over-riding popularity of TV saw less people going to the pictures.

Gateshead Odeon showed its last movie in 1975, and became a Top Rank bingo hall between 1978 and 1995. The building was demolished in 2003.

Newcastle United manager Gordon Lee was at St Mark's Church on Durham Road, Low Fell, Gateshead, in 1975 for the annual prize-giving of Wrekenton Boys' Brigade. The controversial figure, who infamously sold crowd favourite Malcolm Macdonald, briefly held the reins at St James' Park between 1975 and early 1977. Dour and pragmatic, the irony was that Lee guided United to the 1976 League Cup final and, for all intents and purposes, assembled the team which finished fifth in the league - their highest placing since 1951. But that was not before, in late January 1977, he walked out to become manager of Everton, shocking players and fans alike.

Youngsters having fun at Whitley Bay's Spanish City funfair in July 1975. For many born and bred on Tyneside, it was a must-visit location in our formative years – and beyond. The funfair was the subject of the 1981 Dire Straits song Tunnel Of Love.

Youngsters at play in Scotswood, Newcastle, in 1975. The lads were racing 'bogies' – home-made go-carts constructed from old pram wheels and spare bits of wood and rope. In an age before XBox, mobile phones, and health and safety they were great fun.

1976

Long before it became a busy stop on the Tyne and Wear Metro line, Pelaw operated as a railway station. It was one of the many stops on the new rapid transit system that Metro adapted from the old suburban railway lines on the North and South of the River Tyne.

We see the station on June 30, 1976 with graffiti daubed over its walls and buildings. The phenomenon of graffiti was not quite as commonplace when Pelaw railway station opened back in 1843.

It underwent changes in 1850, 1857 and 1896 as Pelaw became home to the Co-operative Wholesale Society at the turn of the 20th century.

The Co-op built an almost mile-long string of red-brick factories along Shields Road on what had been fields between Heworth and Bill Quay. They included a drug and drysaltery works, as well as engineering, cabinet-making, printing, tailoring, shirt, clothing, quilt and bedding factories. Many of the goods that filled the shelves of Co-op "stores" around the North were made here.

When all the factories were operating at their peak, they provided jobs for 3,000 local people, many of whom would have got the train to and from Pelaw.

In 1979 - three years after our graffiti picture was taken - the British Rail station closed, being replaced by Heworth Interchange as a rail stop, with the site also operating as a Metro station when the system began running in 1981.

In 1984, the Metro line was extended down through Hebburn and Jarrow towards South Shields, but it wasn't until the following year that Pelaw opened as a new Metro station. In 2002, when the line to Sunderland opened, the new route branched off just East of Pelaw station.

It was a hot August day in 1976, and a jumble sale was organised by enterprising youngsters at the junction of Elswick Road and St John's Road, in Benwell, Newcastle. It was all in aid of the Evening Chronicle Sunshine Fund, which is still helping children with disabilities and their families today. The original Sunshine Fund was established in 1928 by King George V during his visit to Tyneside. The Chronicle adopted the fund and in 1995 it was granted charitable status when it joined forces with the Community Foundation.

North East workingmen's clubs were still going strong. Beer, bingo and a good 'turn' could be the ingredients for a great night out at the local club. The punters here were enjoying the entertainment at Newcastle's Coxlodge and Gosforth social club on May 30, 1976.

On February 4, 1976, 31 years after the end of World War II, these former members of the Women's Land Army held a reunion at Balmbra's Music Hall in Newcastle's Cloth Market.

A girl sunbathes in the grounds of St John the Baptist church on Newcastle's Westgate Road, and thousands roast on the beach at Tynemouth.

The summer of 1976 was one of the hottest and driest on record. The heatwave kicked off in April and millions of Brits began flocking to the seaside and the countryside, and sunbathing in parks and back gardens.

The summer also delivered a host of problems, however. Droughts, forest fires, hosepipe bans, rising food and beer prices, and the Cabinet considering a three-day week were all big, ongoing stories that hit the headlines that year. The strain on the water system saw a hosepipe ban put in place. One man was fined £5 for watering his back garden.

The then new, and previously criticised, Kielder Reservoir quickly proved to be a saviour for the North East, while standpipes were erected in other parts of the country.

The barley and grain harvest was hit badly and drinkers were warned the price of a pint could rise sharply.

Out in the countryside, one of the major fears was that a stray match or discarded cigarette butt could start an incontrollable inferno in the scorched woodlands and forests of the North. The Newcastle Chronicle took to publishing a daily slogan at the time, one of which read: 'One branch of a tree can produce a million matches – one match can destroy a million trees.'

As week after week of unbroken, blistering weather persisted, Denis Howell, Minister for Sport, was appointed 'minister for drought' – and you could even bet on the chance of rainfall with bookies William Hill.

And then, finally, at the end of August the weather broke and ferocious storms lashed Britain. After four months, the seemingly endless heatwave was over.

In 1976, Newcastle United for once bucked their losing trend in the competition and reached the League Cup final, having disposed of Southport, Bristol Rovers, QPR, Notts County and Spurs on the road to Wembley.

Less than two years after the FA Cup final humiliation at the hands of Kevin Keegan's Liverpool, United had the chance of redemption.

Over 30,000 Geordies headed south to the Twin Towers for the February 28 clash against Tony Book's Manchester City.

Gordon Lee's team, captained on the day by Tommy Craig, gave a better account of themselves than they had done in the 1974 debacle, but in the event there was heartache once again for the travelling black and white hordes.

Peter Barnes gave City the lead after 11 minutes, only for Supermac to set up Alan Gowling for a 35th minute equaliser. It was United's first Wembley goal since 1955. But it was left to City's Newcastle-born former Sunderland winger Dennis Tueart to score the winner on 46 minutes with an eye-catching overhead strike.

If the team - supposedly ravaged by a flu bug - was left wanting, it was the Newcastle United fans even in defeat who, as ever, made the headlines.

As the Chronicle reported: "Their irrepressible exuberance silenced even the Manchester City fans. 'We Nearly Won The Cup', they roared.

"They brought magnanimity to defeat. Instead of rancour there was goodwill for the victors. In place of sour, dour recrimination there was cheerful rejoinder and, everywhere, the sound of Geordie on the roister."

Our post-match report continued: "It began before the match with the unforgettable scene on Wembley Way where the fans surged forward in a black and white tide towards the stadium.

"The chanting had begun then, at least an hour before kick-off."

Such was the fervour of the 1976 Toon Army, The Observer's renowned sports journalist Hugh McIlvanney called them "one of the most extraordinary crowds in British football".

Meanwhile, Magpies captain Tommy Craig told the Chronicle's John Gibson: "I have never felt so choked in my life as I did at the end when our 30,000 fans stood heartbroken but proud and saluted us."

Back on Tyneside two days later, thousands of fans lined the streets of Newcastle - much as they had done two years earlier - to welcome home their heroes who made their way from the Central Station to St James' Park on an open-topped double-decker bus.

Once again the reception was rapturous, but once again the team had returned home without a trophy.

Remembrance Sunday at Newcastle's Eldon Square, November 1976. The World War I memorial of St George and the Dragon - made of Portland stone and bronze - was unveiled by wartime field marshal, Earl Hague in 1923. Decades later, the pleasant open space around the monument would, for a while, become a magnet for Goths and rockers, earning it the nickname 'hippy green'.

Crowds flocked to the newly opened Eldon Square shopping centre, and the so-called "Mushroom" at Bainbridge.

Opened in March 1976, and taking its name from the nearby grand 19th century Newcastle terrace, today it's a Tyneside institution attracting millions of customers every year.

Officially opened by Queen Elizabeth II a year later, it was the region's first major indoor shopping mall, pre-dating Gateshead's Metrocentre by a decade. It symbolised the move from traditional high-street shopping to the American-style retail mall experience.

Britain's biggest shopping centre at the time it was built, it is home to most of the nation's leading retailers and has undergone massive redevelopment and improvement in recent years.

Back in 1976 the Chronicle reported on the "Eldon Square gold rush".

"Tremendous. Fantastic. Amazing. That's what traders are saying about Eldon Square," the newspaper enthused.

"For takings in Newcastle's £60m shopping centre are beyond their wildest dreams — and the complex has just opened.

"Eldon Square's shopping bag army has set the cash tills ringing up an economic extravaganza and store owners are rubbing their hands with glee.

"Now, some are making efforts to increase staff to cope with the rush.

"WH Smith – takings 100% more than they expected. Top Shop — takings double what they thought they would get. Jackson the Tailor — absolutely delighted. Mothercare — happiest with Newcastle. Greggs — they had to send for more bread."

When The Boat Comes In was the first genuinely "Geordie" production for a nationwide TV audience, paving the way for the likes of Auf Wiedersehen, Pet and Byker Grove.

When viewers tuned in to the series for the first time in 1976, they saw former Likely Lad James Bolam as Sgt Jack Ford, a World War I veteran, returning to his poverty-stricken (fictional) home town of Gallowshield in the North East of the 1920s.

A time of economic depression, Jack finds his home town in the grip of decline, unemployment and trade union activists. He soon falls in with the Seaton family – including schoolteacher Jessie, played by Susan Jameson, Bolam's real-life wife – and is determined to make his mark on the world.

The first three series ran from January 8, 1976, to December 15, 1977. The BBC revived the show in 1981, with the fourth series telling the story of Jack Ford as he returned to Britain penniless, after six years spent bootlegging in the United States, and now based in London. The series ended with Ford shot and killed while attempting to deliver guns to the partisans in the Spanish Civil War.

Many will remember the unmistakable theme tune 'Dance Ti Thy Daddy', based on an old folk tune, and sung by Gateshead-born Alex Glasgow.

The show was created by South Shields novelist and writer James Mitchell who assembled an A-list collection of North East writing talent – Tom Hadaway from North Shields and Sid Chaplin from Shildon, County Durham – as well as Alex Glasgow - to pen episodes for the first series.

In January 1976, police were called to Heaton School in Newcastle after 200 female pupils ran amok in protest at the imposition of corporal punishment for girls. "No-one is going to beat my daughter. I've lost sleep over this," one mother told the Newcastle Chronicle, as parents flocked to the school to complain. Three police cars finally arrived to restore order.

Newcastle's Pig and Whistle pub on December 6, 1976. The 1970-built bar in the city's Cloth Market was a long-time favourite haunt of younger Tyneside revellers.

At a time when the shipyards of the Tyne were still in full swing, thousands clocked on for work as normal on Thursday, September 23, 1976.

At Swan Hunter's Neptune yard, more than 500 men were busy putting the finishing touches to the £23m HMS Glasgow - a new Royal Navy destroyer.

Not long after the start of the morning shift, a huge blast shook the shipyard in Walker, Newcastle. Workers looked on in horror as a fireball roared out of the nearly completed 3,500-tonne Type-42 guided-missile vessel, scorching and twisting the steel structure.

In the event, a devastating fire on board HMS Glasgow would have dire consequences.

The Newcastle Chronicle reported: "Eight men were killed and six injured in one of Britain's worst shipyard disasters.

"The top secret guided missile destroyer HMS Glasgow — one of three ultra-sophisticated Type 42 warships built on the Tyne — was being fitted out at Swan Hunter's Neptune Yard at Wallsend.

"The dead men were working on number three and four decks near the machinery control room, part of which is below the ship's water line. One of them had been married only five weeks and another for 11 months.

"The Glasgow — the eighth Royal Navy ship to bear the city's name — was launched in April by Lady Treacher, wife of Admiral Sir John Treacher."

When the alarm went up, 11 fire engines and 75 crew of Tyne-Wear brigade joined the yard team to fight the blaze and rescue workers.

One worker who escaped later said: "It was pure hell down there. It is gutted inside, with water and burnt-out cables everywhere."

A later report confirmed the blaze was started by a welder's torch after gas had been leaking from an oxygen cylinder. An inquest several months later heard almost twice as much oxygen as normal had collected in the lower levels of HMS Glasgow because safety rules had been breached.

Two months after the fire, Swan Hunter was convicted at York Crown Court of three health and safety offences and fined £3,000.

Our photograph shows the finally completed HMS Glasgow leaving the River Tyne on March 8, 1979, two and a half years after the tragedy. The vessel later took part in the 1981-82 Falklands conflict where she was damaged by an Argentine bomb.

After more than 25 years of service the vessel was decommissioned in 2005, and finally broken up in 2009.

Geordie folk-rockers Lindisfarne played three Christmas shows in 1976 at Newcastle City Hall. This image is from their first ever Christmas concert at the famous venue on December 22 that year. The band had scored huge chart hits in the early 1970s with the likes of Lady Eleanor, Meet Me On The Corner and, later in the decade, Run For Home. The shows in 1976 were joyous and hugely successful, with mass audience singalongs and the smell of Newcastle Brown Ale strong in the air. More than four decades later, the Lindisfarne Christmas shows – albeit with a changing line-up – have become an annual North East institution.

St Mary's Church, seen here on November 4, 1976, is a well-known landmark near the Gateshead side of the Tyne Bridge. The town's foremost place of worship, there was a church at this site for 900 years. The last religious service took place in 1979. Since 2008, St Mary's has been a heritage centre, specialising in the history of Gateshead.

Given the seafaring history of our region, it wasn't totally uncommon to see a vessel in trouble off our shores in the rough North Sea.

Indeed, if we take the stretch of water between Whitby and Berwick, there were around 380 recorded shipwrecks between 1740 and 2000.

Happily, the stricken ship photographed on April 19, 1976 was quickly back at sea. The 4,400-ton collier Duncansby Head had beached in dense fog on the soft sand alongside the Groyne lighthouse at South Shields.

It was a time when the North East coalfield was in operation and colliers still shipped coal from staiths on the River Tyne to London and elsewhere.

Thousands of sightseers gathered to see the ship before it re-floated under its own steam.

But early morning strollers and fishermen had dashed for safety when they saw the ship looming through the fog.

The South Tyneside Parks' Superintendent was on the Groyne when the drama began. He told the Newcastle Chronicle: "The fog was dense, then suddenly this huge shape loomed up in front of us and we realised it was a ship's bow."

The ship was backed off the beach by the master and Tyne pilot in bright sunshine eight hours after running aground, and the collier was soon back afloat.

A bit of a spillage … the scene at Hebburn, South Tyneside, where two tankers containing heavy fuel oil overturned, blocking the line on April 8, 1976.

1977

In the summer of 1977, at the peak of his powers and as reigning world heavyweight boxing champion, Muhammad Ali made a sensational visit to Tyneside.

For millions of people, he was the ultimate sporting hero. He was the most famous man on the planet. In the new age of global television, we had been entranced by Ali's supreme charisma and confidence - and willed him to victory in his epic fights against George Foreman and Joe Frazier, among others.

That he was coming to our little corner of the planet - the North East of England - was incredible, and none who saw the great man in the flesh will ever forget it.

In July 1977, to the huge surprise of Johnny Walker, a Whitburn painter and decorator, Ali accepted his invitation to travel from the United States to England to help raise money for his South Shields boxing club. During his four-day stay he visited Newcastle's Pendower Hall Special School and Grainger Park Boys Club. He sparred with local boys and ex-professionals, and played darts at Gypsies Green Stadium in South Shields.

He even tucked into a traditional North East stottie, and attended South Shields' Al-Ahzar Mosque with his wife and baby daughter to have his wedding blessed by the imam.

He was mobbed everywhere he went. When he took an open-top bus tour of Tyneside on Saturday, July 16, tens of thousands took to the streets to see him.

The Newcastle Chronicle reported: "Muhammad Ali continued his own royal tour of Tyneside today with visits to Newcastle and South Shields, having clowned, laughed and cuddled his way into our hearts."

Ali remarked: "I have been in London about five times but never heard of Newcastle till now."

When the 74-year-old died in June 2016, after suffering from Parkinson's Disease for many years, there was a genuine outpouring of grief around the world – not least on Tyneside.

There was major work at Grey's Monument, Newcastle, as tunnelling for the new Metro system and construction of a new station progressed underground. It was January 25, 1977.

The Newcastle Chronicle reported: "Standing on its circular concrete plinth in a sea of mud and contractors' equipment, Grey's Monument in Newcastle conceals a secret. Beneath it is another monument - a circular column of piles runs nearly 40 feet into the earth to prevent Tyneside having a local version of the Leaning Tower of Pisa.

"This unusual technique, called secant piling, is the safest way to ensure Earl Grey neither leans nor topples under the impact of tunnelling for the Metro system."

We see the Queen and Prince Philip at Gypsies Green Stadium, South Shields, in July 1977.

Meanwhile, over in North Shields, residents of Dorking Avenue, on the Meadowell Estate, enjoyed a party.

The Silver Jubilee of Queen Elizabeth II that year was proof of the enduring popularity of the monarchy in Britain. There were street parties and celebrations across the land, and schoolchildren were given commemorative mugs and coins.

During the summer months, the Queen and Prince Philip embarked on a mammoth tour of the country, visiting thirty-six counties across the UK and Northern Ireland.

On July 15, the North East afforded the Royal couple a rapturous reception.

Thousands cheered as the Royal Yacht Britannia sailed into Newcastle Quayside – and thousands more lined the streets as the Queen's limousine wound its way to South Shields and Sunderland.

The once smart railway station at Blaydon was in a state of disrepair when it was photographed on January 19, 1977.

It was in this year that the vandalised station building, built in 1912, was demolished after falling into decline during the previous decade.

Blaydon had actually been recommended for closure under the Beeching Report of 1963, but this never happened and the station continued as an un-staffed stop.

Trains have been running through Blaydon since 1835 when a service ran between the town and Hexham. By the following year, the first ever Trans-Pennine route between Blaydon and Carlisle was under way.

Those early services, hauled by locomotives Rapid and Comet, were eventful affairs with derailments of some of the coaches, but the line soon settled down to provide a reliable link between the North East, North West and beyond.

Much later, just before the vandalised station buildings were demolished in 1977, one railway enthusiast even referred to Blaydon as "probably Britain's least attractive station".

Today, regular daily services stop at a very different Blaydon railway station.

Shoppers were out in force on Gosforth High Street, Newcastle, on March 24, 1977. Then, as now, Gosforth was one of Tyneside's more prosperous suburbs. The High Street was, until relatively recently, part of the trunk route A1 stretching from London to Edinburgh. Since 1988 the main North to South road has by-passed the west and north of the city, and the High Street is now just a local route. The name Gosforth is said to derive from Roman times when it was known as "Goose Ford".

Drinkers in the Printer's Pie pub, Pudding Chare, Newcastle in 1977. The bar – later renamed Fleet Street – was a long-time favourite with newspaper staff who worked at the adjoining Thomson House, home of the Chronicle, Journal and Sunday Sun between 1965 and 2018.

Newcastle United fans of a certain vintage will remember scenes like this.

This was the famous Gallowgate End at St James' Park on a match day in 1977. From these terraces, generations of fans watched United's ups and downs.

The famous 'end' began life as an earth bank as the club established itself in the 1890s. In the 1930s, United pressed ahead with plans replacing the St James' ash and wood terracing with concrete.

And if Gallowgate End regulars had to cope with whatever the weather threw at them, plans to build a roof in the late 1920s were dropped after endless planning wrangles.

For those of us who stood on the jam-packed Gallowgate terrace in our younger days, it could be exhilarating, raucous and very tribal.

But by the 1980s and 90s, the Gallowgate End was a tatty stretch of terracing well past its sell-by date. Not content with primitive toilet facilities, full-on exposure to the vicissitudes of the Tyneside weather, and the pushing, crushing and general argy-bargy of a terraced crowd, you were on your hind legs for 90 minutes-plus. It was not a great customer experience.

The Gallowgate End terraces finally bowed out after the 1993-94 season and were demolished to make way for the new, 21st century St James' Park.

The North Eastern Co-op on Newcastle's Newgate Street was all done up on July 12, 1977 for the imminent visit of the Queen to the region on her Silver Jubilee tour.

Between 1932 and 2011, it attracted shoppers from across the region. It was the Co-op's in-house architect LG Ekins who designed the new store, employing many art deco features – inside and out – that characterised the inter-war period.

With its twin towers, sweeping curves and huge windows boasting impressive views across the city, the now-iconic building was once seen as Newcastle's most elegant shopping outlet. Across 170,000 sq ft and housed on six floors, linked by marble-lined staircases, it was the ultimate retail experience.

In February 2016, the building – retaining many of its original features – reopened as a 184-bed Premier Inn after a five-year £17m revamp.

1977 saw Newcastle Brown Ale celebrating its 50th birthday.

It was Colonel Jim Porter who, in 1924, came up with the recipe for the region's most famous tipple.

On April 25, 1927, Newcastle Brown Ale was advertised for sale for the first time in The Journal newspaper. Five days later, Newcastle United were crowned league champions – their last title to date! The blue star logo was introduced to Newcastle Brown Ale bottles in 1928.

In the 1970s – and indeed before and after – the not unpleasant smell of brewing beer regularly wafted over the city.

In 2005, the beer's manufacture was moved from Newcastle to the Federation Brewery in Gateshead. And in 2010, it controversially moved out of the North East to Tadcaster in North Yorkshire.

Today the famous Brown Ale is brewed by Heineken at the Zoeterwoude Brewery in Holland. Its spiritual home, however, will always be Newcastle.

On May 6, 1977, the recently-installed US President, Jimmy Carter arrived on Tyneside for a very high-profile visit.

The Democrat governor and so-called 'peanut farmer from Georgia' had assumed the role of the world's most powerful man in January of that year, and an official visit to Tyneside formed part of his first foreign trip.

Carter's wife, Rosalynn, had launched the Friendship Force to build bridges between the US and the rest of the world. One of the first cities to become involved was Newcastle, and exchanges involving 762 travellers were due to take place with Atlanta. Those involved would stay in each other's homes, experience each other's jobs, and learn about life in a foreign country.

The President, accompanied by Labour Prime Minister Jim Callaghan, was given a rapturous reception after landing at Newcastle Airport in Air Force One.

Famously, in front of a 20,000-strong crowd outside Newcastle Civic Centre, he uttered the Geordie phrase "Howay the Lads" during his speech, before heading to Washington Old Hall, the stone-built mansion that was the ancestral home of America's first president, George Washington.

Carter made a return trip to Newcastle, 10 years after his first visit.

Workers finish their shift at Swan Hunter shipyard, Wallsend, on November 29, 1977.

But these were troubled times. This was the year nationalisation saw British Shipbuilders take over the Tyne's larger yards, as the domestic industry struggled with shrinking order books, and Korea and Japan began to produce cheaper ships.

This was Whitley Bay's popular Spanish City fairground in June 1977.

The unmistakable structure with its spectacular dome, opened in May, 1910 – days after the death of King Edward VII. The original pleasure palace had a 1,400-seat concert hall, restaurant, roof garden and tearoom. A ballroom was added in 1920, a decade when Whitley Bay was advertised as the 'Blackpool of the North East'.

The first fairground had operated since 1908, and soon attracted thousands of visitors every day.

The origins of the 'Spanish City' name came from a travelling 'Toreadors' concert party who performed in a temporary Spanish-style painted stage set in 1907. The popular act returned to Whitley Bay each summer and it was decided that a permanent amusement park was needed to be created.

The middle decades of the last century saw the Spanish City's heyday. The Corkscrew roller coaster arrived as a national first in the 1980s, bringing with it a new generation of funseekers.

The complex closed in 1999. In the summer of 2018, the Spanish City was reborn as a multi-million pound leisure hub.

If 1977 was the year when the Krypton Factor, Citizen Smith and Robin's Nest, among others, first appeared on our TV screens, so did another offering made closer to home.

Tyne Tees TV launched the drama series The Paper Lads, telling of the ups and downs of a group of teenage news deliverers on Tyneside. The show was first screened on August 24, 1977, and came to an end two years later.

Largely shot on location, mainly in Gateshead, there were two series made, each with seven episodes.

The theme tune, Back Home Once Again, was performed by the progressive rock band Renaissance. The song includes the memorable lyric "making our entrance and reading the lines, the story of people who live by the Tyne".

Well-known character actor Glynn Edwards, who'd appeared in the cult Geordie gangster flick, Get Carter, played former policeman turned newsagent, Jack Crawford. Edwards would go on to play Dave, the barman at the Winchester Club in the smash TV hit, Minder.

Scripts were by County Durham-born actor Ian Cullen, who was well known for playing Joe Skinner in the iconic BBC police drama Z-Cars. Each episode of the Paper Lads told of the adventures of the boys - and girl - on their rounds.

The show was described by Tyne Tees as "a nice, lively blend of excitement, drama and humour, and definitely for all ages".

(Top) Let's hope these two ladies didn't wait too long for their bus at Newcastle's Marlborough Crescent station on January 10, 1977. From the signs close by, we can tell they were heading towards Stanley or Consett.

Indeed, Marlborough Crescent station, built in the late-1920s, served bus passengers travelling into North West Durham, Cumberland, Westmoreland, and all points west along the Tyne Valley, including Carlisle, for around 60 years. The oldest of the city's stations, the last bus would set off from here in the late 1980s.

Elsewhere in the city, bus services from Worswick Street station (which operated between 1929 and 1998) would generally head to the South of the region. And buses to the North and East started their journeys at Haymarket station, which is still going strong.

Today, there is no trace of Marlborough Crescent bus station. In 2000, the pioneering Centre for Life was opened on the site of the station and a patch of derelict industrial land next to Newcastle Central Station.

(Middle)If punk rock burned brightly but briefly in the late 1970s, one band that is still revered is The Clash.

Their lyrics were topical and political. And their range of musical styles - ska, rockabilly and dub, as well as punk - would separate them from their contemporaries.

Our photograph captures the band in action in Newcastle on May 20, 1977.

But before that, one gig that might have happened at Newcastle City Hall, but never did, had been due to take place on December 5, 1976.

The Sex Pistols, The Damned and The Clash were all due in the city on the Anarchy In The UK tour, but most of the shows - including Newcastle - were cancelled due to the furore that followed the Pistols' infamous TV clash with Bill Grundy.

Five months later, on their White Riot tour, the Clash - Joe Strummer, Mick Jones, Paul Simenon and Topper Headon - rolled up for a show at Newcastle University's students' union bar.

The gig was somewhat chaotic, but the band powered through a short set that included London's Burning, Police and Thieves, and White Riot - their first single.

Punk was a new, raw phenomenon, as was the audience spitting frenzy which left Strummer and co drenched.

Meanwhile, the ticket-only crowd was made up mainly of students, while punks outside fought running battles with doormen as they tried to get in.

After the show it was even reported two members of the band were fined - for stealing hotel towels and pillows!

1977 was the start of a momentous journey for the Clash who would finally split in 1986. Joe Strummer passed away in 2002.

(Bottom) Opened by the Queen on October 19, 1967, this was the Tyne Tunnel, running under the River Tyne from Jarrow in South Tyneside to Howdon in North Tyneside on August 31, 1977. Today this is the northbound tunnel. Southbound traffic uses a second tunnel, opened in 2011.

1978

The Metro Bridge is one of the less famous of the River Tyne's iconic crossings, but it has been integral to the region's transport infrastructure for four decades. Built in the mid-to-late-1970s, the QEII Bridge was the most vital engineering solution in the long-awaited development of the Metro.

Here we see it under construction in 1978. It was an historic project, connecting Newcastle and Gateshead with a light railway system, which became the envy of other cities.

The QEII Bridge, the sixth across the Tyne, was officially named by Her Majesty the Queen on November 6, 1981, as part of the official Royal opening of the Metro system. The opening was part of a three-week transport festival on Tyneside, designed to encourage people to try the Metro.

There was a fireworks display, a transport treasure trail, competitions - including one with a first prize of a Spanish holiday - a balloon race, a public transport cavalcade and exhibition, specially commissioned souvenirs and cheap fares.

The first Metro trains in passenger service actually crossed the bridge in August 1980 when the Metro system first started running.

When construction started in 1976 it was quickly decided that trains should cross the river on a 368-metre bridge, rather than in tunnels dug beneath the river. The river bed was excavated and two concrete abutments were built to support the steel.

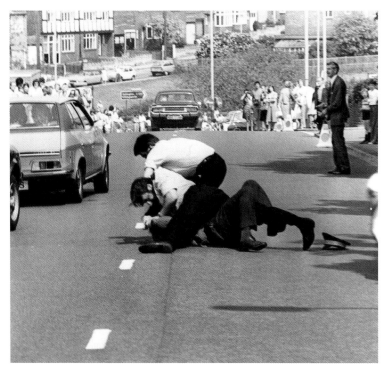

A moment of drama during the visit of Prince Charles to Newcastle on May 31, 1978. Moments after leaving the city's newly-opened Freeman Hospital, the prince's car was attacked by a man throwing a bottle. Police and security men were instantly on the scene. The man was bundled to the ground and arrested, while the unruffled prince continued with his visit.

It was June 20, 1978, when five sailors from HMS Newcastle were photographed on Newcastle Quayside, having completed a 360-mile charity bike ride from Portsmouth. The Royal Navy Type-42 Destroyer had been launched at Swan Hunter's Neptune yard at Low Walker, Newcastle, in April 1975. The so-called 'Geordie Gunboat' would be decommissioned in February 2005, and scrapped four years later.

The giant cranes at Wallsend's Swan Hunter shipyard were hard at work in December 1978. Under construction was the aircraft carrier, HMS Illustrious.

The vessel, known to her crew as Lusty Lady, had slid gracefully into the Tyne after being officially launched by Princess Margaret earlier in the month. The official launching ceremony at Swan Hunter, Wallsend, was watched by the 3,000 workers who finished the ship well ahead of schedule.

The size of the vessel was impressive, with a length of 636ft, a beam of 118ft, and a displacement of 22,000 tonnes.

The royal launch in 1978 was merely ceremonial, and the serious business of fitting out the ship over several years would then begin.

The Falklands War of 1982, however, meant work on Illustrious needed to be speeded up so the carrier could join the conflict in the South Atlantic. Finishing the job three months early, the expertise of the Swans' workforce was praised by the visiting boss of British Shipbuilding, Mr Robert Atkinson, in May 1982.

Finally, in the midst of one of the most dramatic periods in Britain's recent history, it was reported in August 1982 that Illustrious had arrived in the Falklands to help in the aftermath of the conflict.

Illustrious would not be formally commissioned until March 1983.

The ship had a range of 5,000 miles, the distance from Newcastle to San Francisco, and needed 400 tonnes of fresh water every day to meet the demands of the crew.

In the decades that followed, the vessel was involved in conflicts in Iraq, Bosnia and Sierra Leone, as well as countless NATO exercises around the globe. After more than three decades of active service, HMS Illustrious was decommissioned in August 2014.

It was the best-attended match at St James' Park during 1978 – and it didn't feature Newcastle United!

Football fans from all corners of our region joined forces to back the thrilling exploits of non-league Blyth Spartans.

The bitterly cold night of Monday, February 27, 1978, was one of the few occasions when Newcastle United and Sunderland fans stood shoulder-to-shoulder backing the same cause at St James' Park.

As for the Magpies' own season, 1977-78 was particularly wretched. After beating Leeds in the opening game of the league campaign, they conspired to lose the next 10 matches on the bounce. A dismal relegation beckoned.

And in the FA Cup, United suffered a second-round 4-1 humbling at Third Division Wrexham as the season limped from crisis to crisis.

It was left to little Blyth Spartans to illuminate the footballing gloom.

To recap, the magnificent non-leaguers had seen off four local sides in the qualifying rounds of that season's FA Cup.

Then, in the first round proper, fellow part-timers Burscough were disposed of, before Spartans beat third division Chesterfield in the second round, and minnows Enfield in the third round. Their reward? An away tie at Stoke City.

Incredibly, the North East outfit triumphed 3-2 against a side fielding the likes of Howard Kendall, Terry Conroy, and a young Garth Crooks.

Had Newcastle not crumbled to an infamous defeat against Wrexham, Blyth would have earned a fairy-tale clash against their illustrious Magpie neighbours.

In the event, Spartans faced the Welshmen at the Racecourse Ground only to controversially concede a last-minute equaliser after the referee ordered a Wrexham corner to be retaken three times.

The replay, would take place not at Blyth's Croft Park, but at St James' Park. With the Toon in freefall, home attendances had plummeted to around 20,000.

But on that night, 42,000 were at Gallowgate to create an awesome wall of noise. Thousands more were locked out at a time when most matches were pay-at-the-gate.

Blyth were 2-0 down in 20 minutes and, despite pulling a late goal back, and with the huge baying crowd providing deafening support, Spartans bowed out.

Work for the new Metro system was still ongoing below and above ground level at the Monument, Newcastle in August 1978. It was another two years before the region-wide transport system would open.

Meanwhile, the long-gone New Sunrise Chinese Restaurant was a popular city centre eating place.

Newcastle's Grainger Market is one of the city's most famous locations. Its shops, stalls, cafes and its unique hustle and bustle have been an integral part of Tyneside life for generations. Here we see the indoor market in 1978.

In October, 1835, 2,000 men sat down to a celebratory opening dinner in the market. For five shillings, wealthier attendees could enjoy fine food, a pint of wine and the sounds of a band.

(Women, however, were only allowed to watch proceedings from a specially built temporary gallery!)

The Grainger Market is today owned and operated by Newcastle City Council and still forms an important commercial and social hub in the city centre. The market is Grade-1 listed, employs 800 people, and attracts thousands of shoppers to more than 100 retail units every week.

Quite probably, the region's most photographed object – the Tyne Bridge. Here we see the iconic structure on July 9, 1978.

While the bridge is still much very present and correct – and has been since 1928 – this particular corner of the Quayside has changed since our image was captured. The Shell petrol outlet is no more, as is the branch of Lloyds Bank.

The city centre has lost a host of banks over recent decades as technology has changed the way we deal with our money. The use of plastic cards and internet banking has lessened the need for bricks and mortar banks.

Many of the old buildings have been repurposed. Stroll around Newcastle's Grey Street and Grainger Street these days and there are often pints and pizzas for sale in buildings in which we used to cash cheques and deposit money.

For those who hail from the North East and are of a certain age, the annual Tyneside Summer Exhibition will evoke fond memories. It was hugely popular.

Running from 1963 to 1987 in Newcastle's Exhibition Park, it was spread over five days, Tuesday to Saturday, and it had five main component sections.

The "family entertainment" section featured the likes of the Red Arrows team, the Parachute Regiment, Army motorcycle teams and the regimental band of the Blues and Royals. There were also local pipe bands and contests for juvenile jazz bands to thrill the crowds.

A general trades section, housed in a marquee, 500ft by 90ft, hosted a state-of-the-art display of domestic utilities, fridges, freezers, cookers, home improvements, DIY, leisure clothing, with all sorts of stalls selling pretty much everything under the sun.

The agricultural section, under the umbrella of the Wansbeck Society, included cattle, sheep and horse displays, with full-day arena events on the Royal Show site, featuring sheepdogs, show jumping and pony gymkhanas being particularly popular.

There was a National Farmers Union section where another large marquee hosted home-produced foods, fashion parades - of usually wool-based garments - and cookery demonstrations which, like the fashion shows, were extremely popular.

And there was also the city flower show, first held in 1947. By the 1960s, there was £1,500 in prize money, attracting 20 large growers, plus over 1,000 entries in various amateur classes.

Here we see members of the Royal Navy display team giving a gymnastic exhibition, 35 feet above the ground at the exhibition on August 4, 1978.

Generations of North East revellers flocked to this location. This was Tiffany's nightclub in Newcastle, in September 1978.

Over the decades it was also known as Ritzy, Ikon, The Studio, Central Park, Diva, Liquid Envy, and Club LQ. But its best-known incarnation was the Oxford Galleries.

The dance hall on Newcastle's New Bridge Street opened in 1925. The building dated from 1825 and was originally the home of John Dobson, the architectural genius who helped transform Newcastle.

Who knows how many couples met, danced, and kissed at the popular venue before tying the knot?

In 2015, marking the end of an era, it was reported the old Oxford Galleries building would be transformed into student accommodation for 305 people.

This was Newcastle's trendiest Nightclub, Tuxedo Junction, in June, 1978. It was opened by flamboyant Newcastle businessman Michael Quadrini just as the disco craze arrived and Saturday Night Fever took over the cinemas and pop charts. In its day, Tuxedo Junction attracted everyone from Princess Margaret to showbiz personality Hughie Green, and Kevin Keegan to actor Lewis Collins of TV's The Professionals. Mr Quadrini would later open the two floating nightclubs on the River Tyne, the Tuxedo Princess and the Tuxedo Royale.

Skateboarding at the Lightfoot Stadium in Walker, Newcastle on February 26, 1978. The skateboard phenomenon began in the United States in the 1940s and 50s, reaching the UK a few decades later. It was all the rage in the 1970s.

The 1970s - and more and more of us began to jet off abroad on package holidays. Here we see passengers waiting to depart from a busy Newcastle Airport on July 30, 1978. The airport was officially opened on July 26, 1935, by Secretary of State for Air, Sir Phillip Cunliffe-Lister. The first scheduled domestic service calling at Newcastle Airport was a flight between Croydon and Perth, Scotland, operated by North Eastern Airways using an 8-seater Airspeed Envoy aircraft. The 1970s began with Newcastle becoming the ninth busiest of Britain's 39 airports with 416,000 annual passengers.

A young Steve Cram in action at the Jarrow and Hebburn round table sports day, July 15, 1978. The middle distance runner – nicknamed the 'Jarrow Arrow' – would go on to win the 1,500 metres Olympic silver in 1984, and break numerous world records. Monkton Stadium, in Jarrow, is still known to older folk by its former name, the Metupa. Its name derived from the town's three main employers who financed its creation – Jarrow Metals, Tube Works, and Palmer's.

Eager customers pile into a new branch of Dicksons the butcher in Wallsend, North Tyneside in 1978. Famed for its belly-busting saveloy dips, pork butcher Dicksons began life as a single shop in South Shields in 1953. The firm was aiming to have 40 stores operating by June 2019.

Now, at first glance, this looks serious. The photograph was taken on May 17, 1978. It captured an incident on the escalator descending to the Tyne pedestrian and cycle tunnels.

A dramatic Newcastle Chronicle report from that day read: "Three people lie dead at the foot of an escalator.

"Thirty others are seriously hurt in a tangle of bruised and broken bodies – a slip on the steep moving stairway has led to this tragedy.

"However, fortunately, this was only a mock-up to aid the emergency services who may need to attend this type of accident in the future."

The tunnel – which is today Grade II-listed – runs under the River Tyne from Howdon in North Tyneside to Jarrow in South Tyneside.

It opened on July 24, 1951, and was Tyneside's contribution to the nationwide Festival of Britain celebrations that year.

At the time of writing, the tunnel has been closed for major works for five years.

This was the end of the notorious Noble Street housing estate in Newcastle's West End. Built in the late 1950s, it lasted only 20 years after being blighted by social problems, vandalism, and a high crime rate. It was nicknamed 'Alcatraz' by local residents. The wrecking ball crashes against the flats at the beginning of the demolition programme on August 15, 1978.

1979

This is one of Tyneside's steepest hills - and on January 30, 1979, its descent was particularly icy and treacherous. More than 20 buses were forced to pull up and discharge their passengers as it was deemed too dangerous to drive any further.

We're looking at Sheriffs Highway, part of the Old Durham Road, in Gateshead. The area today is largely unchanged and, from this highest point in Tyneside, there are spectacular northward views into Newcastle and beyond. On clear days you can see the Cheviots.

From the 13th century, Sheriff Hill was where the sheriffs from Newcastle would come to meet and escort the judges from Durham as they travelled to hold assizes in Newcastle. Until the 20th century, the road had a less salubrious name - Sodhouse Bank.

A couple of centuries ago, this area was little more than barren, wind-swept moorland, with scattered houses and cottages bisected by the rough road leading to Newcastle. Meanwhile, nearby Beacon Lough had been home to a series of warning beacons established in Queen Elizabeth I's reign. The last one blew down in 1808.

Newcastle's Central Motorway in 1979. Since it opened in 1973, it has become a vital route for anyone trying to navigate the city. The Central Motorway was built in response to the huge rise in traffic on our roads from the early 1950s onwards. The original plans included a Central Motorway East and West, but these were shelved due to cost concerns, and, later, environmental ones.

La Dolce Vita nightclub, on Newcastle's Low Friar Street, was one of the city's most notable nightspots. We see it here in July, 1979 when it was well past its sell-by date.

The brainchild of three Wallsend businessmen brothers – David, Marcus and Norman Levey – it opened in February 6, 1963. The Kaye Sisters were the first act to perform, followed by Matt Monro, Alma Cogan and Dickie Valentine, and soon the Dolce was as famous in the North as London's Talk of the Town was in the capital.

Showbiz stars flocked to the region. They would be flown over from America to perform for a week or a fortnight at the Talk of the Town, and then travel North to sing or crack jokes in the Toon. The acts were brought into the club at affordable prices, subsidised by profits from its roulette and blackjack tables.

Billy Daniels, Mel Torme and Billy Eckstein all performed, along with up-and-coming young British acts like Helen Shapiro, Cilla Black and Manfred Mann. Ella Fitzgerald insisted on going to the Dolce after her gig at Newcastle City Hall, and other stars to pass through its doors included The Beatles, Shirley Bassey, Jackie and Joan Collins, and Adam Faith.

Tom Jones was just 25 when he appeared at the Dolce Vita in 1965, and a young David Frost even had to face hecklers as a stand-up comic at the club. Bob Monkhouse, who went on to own his own Newcastle nightclub, Change Is, (formerly the Casablanca) in Bath Lane, was also a firm favourite at La Dolce Vita.

But with the glamour came a darker side. London mobsters Ronnie and Reggie Kray visited as they tried to extend their empire in the mid-1960s. And La Dolce Vita was made notorious in 1967 when it was named in the Angus Sibbet gangland killing case dubbed the 'One-Armed Bandit Murder' by the press.

The Levey brothers sold the club in 1967 to the Bailey Organisation, which turned out to be a shrewd move as the Gaming Act came into being in 1968. It meant entertainment had to be separated from gaming - and clubs could no longer afford to pay the top acts.

La Dolce Vita fell into a slow decline which saw it move from attracting a star-studded clientele to, in 1979, announcing that it offered 'The Cheapest Beer on Tyneside' at 29p a pint.

Rescue came in the shape of Malcolm and Bill Walker, who bought the club and re-opened it as Walker's in 1984. It hit the headlines in 1991 when footballer Paul Gascoigne's knee was injured in an incident there.

In 1993 Absolute Leisure took over, re-named the club Planet Earth and refurbished the interior, giving the venue a new lease of life as a dance club.

In 2001 the club had yet another re-fit and was reopened as The Playrooms. This was to be the last hurrah of the old La Dolce Vita venue. Staff who turned up for work on November 15, 2002, found the doors in Low Friar Street locked.

The club was re-built into luxury flats and, along with the nearby, and much-missed Mayfair, it has become one of Tyneside's great lost nightspots.

A busy Shields Road, Byker, Newcastle in 1979. Long before the shops plied their trade here from the 19th century, the place had its roots in the mists of time. The place name 'Byker' translates as a village next to a marsh (kerr) in old Norse.

Ladies competing in the Shrove Tuesday Jiff Lemon's Pancake Race in Clayton Street, Newcastle on February 21, 1979. Much changed over time, the street was named after John Clayton, the long-serving Town Clerk and antiquarian who helped builder Richard Grainger ease past various legal issues as he pursued his grand vision of a new Newcastle. Mainly consisting of shops and houses, it was one of the final parts of Grainger's radical redevelopment of Newcastle , and was completed in 1841.

People flocking to Newcastle Quayside's Sunday Market in March 1979. In the background, on the other side of the River Tyne, Gateshead's Baltic flour mill was still in operation, some 23 years before it became a modern art gallery.

Whatever became of these girls? These were the 21 Miss Newcastle contestants on July 25, 1979. The winner would gain entry into the Miss UK contest the following month. In the worldly-wise 21st century the notion of beauty contests might seem politically incorrect and old-fashioned to some, but they were still going strong in the 1970s. The Miss World competition had been launched by Eric Morley in 1951 as part of that year's Festival of Britain celebrations. But as far back as 1905, Newcastle was hosting an event called the Blonde and Brunette Beauty Show - open to girls over 16 - at the city's Olympia Theatre.

These Newcastle revellers were strutting their stuff at a Newcastle nightclub in October, 1979. The disco phenomenon had been building from the mid-70s then exploded in 1978 after the release of the film Saturday Night Fever, starring John Travolta. The soundtrack album was seemingly immovable at the top of the album charts as disco music reigned. Written largely by the Bee Gees, the record boasted classics such as Stayin' Alive, How Deep Is Your Love and Night Fever. The band also penned hits for Yvonne Elliman and Tavares on this multi-platinum offering.

Go to a pop concert these days and you'll more than likely be able to book your tickets online with the press of a few keyboard buttons. In the 1970s, you would often have to queue – sometimes overnight – if a big name came to town. On February 2, 1979, around 40 Elton John fans spent the night in sub-zero temperatures to make sure of getting tickets for the superstar singer's upcoming concerts at Newcastle City Hall on March 22 and 23.

It's something you just don't see today. Dogs on the pitch at football matches!

There have, in fact, been a handful of daring canine pitch invaders over the years at St James' Park, the most notable being 'Shep', a black-and-white collie-type who decided to enter the field of play during a match in late 1979.

Shep somehow found himself among a crowd of just over 25,000 on a chilly December 15 that year as Newcastle United hosted Queens Park Rangers. Bill McGarry's United side were top of Division Two as Christmas approached, but their promotion bid would go off the rails as the season progressed.

As for the QPR game, Shep couldn't resist joining in the action as a Newcastle team featuring Tommy Cassidy, Terry Hibbitt, Alan Shoulder and Peter Withe earned a 4-2 win. It was the muscular Withe who made an unsuccessful lunge for the dog which was happily running around the Gallowgate End 18-yard box.

Two burly policemen finally collared the pitch interloper and brought a swift end to his United career.

The number 25 bus to Wrekenton trundles down Newcastle's main shopping thoroughfare, Northumberland Street, on July 24, 1979. The opening of Fenwick's store on its current site in 1885 was a key moment in the development of the modern street. By 1914 and the outbreak of World War I, 400 people worked there. There was a further retail boom in the street in 1932 when Marks and Spencer and C&A moved in. Northumberland Street was finally reclaimed from the heavy traffic and pedestrianised in 1998.

A gritty shot of Hebburn railway station in 1979. The arrival of the railway in 1872 helped the town thrive and expand in the 19th century – and beyond.

During the 20th century, Hebburn's fortunes were in the hands of modern engineering companies such as Reyrolle, established in 1901, and Hawthorn Leslie shipbuilder which had operated from the 1850s.

Like many of its neighbours, the town suffered from the ups and downs of the economy, but it also benefited from slum clearance and the construction of a new civic centre in the post-war era. Today the town is a location for many new private housing projects.

Hebburn railway station closed in June, 1981 and reopened as a refurbished station on the Tyne and Wear Metro system in March, 1984.

Lindisfarne are one of the most successful groups to emerge from the North East. The band enjoyed a string of folk-infused hit singles and albums during the 1970s. Their most well-known song is probably Fog on the Tyne and, appropriately enough, here they are aboard a ferry on the River Tyne recording a song for the Tyne Tees music show, All Right Now in March, 1979.

The North East is littered with 1960s and 70s housing experiments that failed - and this is one of them.

However well-intentioned St Cuthbert's Village in Gateshead was, it stood for just 25 years before the last bulldozers moved in. It was built on the steep North-facing incline of Windmill Hills overlooking the River Tyne. The estate replaced the sloping Victorian-built terraced streets that once straddled Askew Road and were deemed as slums and earmarked for demolition by the 1960s.

The cost of the ambitious project was £3.5m, and 3,500 Gateshead folk would be housed. The village was formally opened by Labour Prime Minister Harold Wilson on April 17, 1970.

By the 1980s, St Cuthbert's had a reputation as a location rife with anti-social behaviour, deprivation and a decaying housing stock. In 1995, the last of the 470 flats was demolished, although the tower block, St Cuthbert's Court, remains today.

It was December 14, 1979 and the battered 400-ton coaster Ganton lay stranded, having run aground on rocks near St Mary's Island, Whitley Bay. It was reported how the Tynemouth lifeboat was called out to take the four crew members to safety. The vessel was later freed from the rocks at high tide.

A shipyard workers' union meeting at Hebburn, 1979. By then, shipbuilding was still a going concern on the River Tyne but under severe pressure from cheaper foreign competition.

Hebburn's famous Hawthorn Leslie shipyard began operation in 1853. During the boom years of the early 20th century, the yard list shows a great variety of vessels - passenger ships, early oil tankers, British and foreign naval vessels and great lake steamers - were built at Hebburn.

The most famous ship constructed at the yard was the ill-fated HMS Kelly, launched in 1938 and commanded by Lord Louis Mountbatten. The proud vessel was sunk by the Luftwaffe with the loss of half the crew in May 1941, during the evacuation of Crete in World War II.

The Hawthorn Leslie yard, having plodded on under different guises, suffered the same fate as other Tyne shipyards as the 21st century dawned. Work stopped there in the early 2000s, and its old buildings would stand empty and derelict for years.

The winter of 1978-79 is on record as one of the worst ever in the UK. As 1979 began, the country was engulfed by crippling blizzards and deep snow. Here we see idle rail tracks as adverse weather conditions hit Newcastle Central Station on February 16, 1979.

Labour Prime Minister Jim Callaghan found himself with a 60% popularity rating in 1978, before widespread public sector strikes culminated in the 'winter of discontent', bringing hardship and shortages across the country. Here we see rubbish piling up on the pavement of Shakespeare Street, Newcastle, during a strike by binmen in March 1979. Two months later, the Conservative party, under Margaret Thatcher, ousted Labour and swept to power. Thatcher's government would preside throughout the 1980s, a decade that would deliver a whole host of real problems for Newcastle and Tyneside – but that's another story.